THE DICTATORSHIP SYNDROME

ABOUT THE AUTHOR

Alaa Al Aswany was born in 1957. A dentist by profession, he is the author of the bestselling novels *The Yacoubian Building*, *Chicago*, *The Automobile Club of Egypt*, the novella and short story collection *Friendly Fire* and the 2011 non-fiction work *On the State of Egypt*. His work has been translated into 37 languages and published in over 100 countries. Al Aswany was named by *The Times* as one of the best 50 authors to have been translated into English in the last 50 years.

THE DICTATORSHIP SYNDROME

ALAA AL ASWANY

Translated by Russell Harris

First published in 2019 by
HAUS PUBLISHING LTD
4 Cinnamon Row
London SW11 3TW
www.hauspublishing.com

This first paperback edition published in 2021

A CIP catalogue record for this book is available from the British Library

ISBN: 978-1-913368-04-3
eISBN: 978-1-912208-60-9

Typeset in Garamond by MacGuru Ltd

Printed in the United Kingdom by TJ Books Limited, Padstow

Contents

Author's note   vii

1 The syndrome   1
2 Symptoms of the dictatorship syndrome   15
3 The emergence of the good citizen   27
4 The conspiracy theory   37
5 The spread of the fascist mindset   47
6 The dislocation of the intellectual   65
7 Dictatorship and the predisposing factors
   for terrorism   85
8 The course of the syndrome   105
9 Prevention of the dictatorship syndrome   133

Notes   145
Acknowledgements   173
Index   175

Author's note

I first made the acquaintance of Barbara Schwepcke some years ago when she was introduced to me by another dear friend, the now late Mark Linz, Director of the American University in Cairo Press. Barbara was Mark's partner both in life and professionally, and we three used to meet quite often in Cairo, London and Frankfurt. We would spend long hours discussing what was happening in the world, particularly in Egypt, a country that both Mark and Barbara loved. Over time, I discovered that Barbara was driven by a personal commitment to defending freedom everywhere and that she used book publishing as a weapon against ignorance, authoritarianism and indeed against anything that deprived people of their human rights. When the Egyptian revolution broke out in 2011, Barbara gave it her wholehearted support. She travelled to Cairo and went to Tahrir Square to listen to what people were saying. She spoke to everyone she knew about the revolution and its inherent risks. She was as supportive of the revolution as any Egyptian revolutionary.

Three years later, when General Abdel Fattah el-Sisi took power, my work was blacklisted in Egypt. Around the same time, I suggested to Barbara that she might publish all my articles about the revolution in book form. She held the view that my novels had already been translated into various languages and that my fiction was well known, but that my articles also needed to be made accessible to a non-Arab readership. She told me that no one could prevent me from publishing my thoughts and that the best response to my being blacklisted would be to publish a collection of my articles. Barbara decided that the title of the book should be "Democracy is the Answer", which was the refrain with which I finished all my articles. The book was published in London to positive acclaim from the English readership.

Some months later, I came up with another suggestion for Barbara: that she should hold a series of discussions with me about the phenomenon of dictatorship in the twentieth century, which could then be published as a book. She was enthusiastic about the idea, and we started to have regular conversations, recorded by her two assistants. Barbara – a woman of great culture – had an astonishing talent in directing the debate. Our conversation ended up touching on other related topics of significance, and I started to look for signs of dictatorship in humanity in general. What was the difference between a youth who has grown up in China or Egypt and a youth of the same educational level in Britain or America? How do traces of dictatorial attitudes find their way into the behaviour of the everyday citizen?

I will always remember the evening I was sitting in my room in the Gore Hotel in London. I was doing some reading before the next day's debating session, when a new thought came to me. The next morning, I told Barbara that the subject of our discussions was too weighty and that a debate might not be the best way to present it to the public.

I said that I wanted to write about the subject as a series of articles instead. She agreed on the spot and suggested, there and then, that I should write my study of dictatorship in the form of a medical report entitled "The Dictatorship Syndrome".

My dear friend and literary agent Charles Buchan found the concept exciting and had a contract speedily drawn up. We all agreed that Russell Harris, an accomplished translator, should be asked to transpose the text into English.

I started work on the book immediately and finished around half of it in Cairo. My relationship with the Egyptian regime had by then deteriorated to the point where my presence in my own country represented a threat both to me and to members of my family, so I copied the half-finished book onto a USB flash drive and hid it between the toothpaste and shaving cream in my washbag as I left the country. Whenever I enter or exit Egypt, the authorities pull me to one side and make me wait as they go through my suitcase twice before letting me go. Had they found material for a book, they would have confiscated it and had it examined by a committee of officers and I would then have, most probably, been hauled off to court and seen levelled against me yet another charge of "slandering the institutions of state".

This kind of censorship is just one of the many reasons why I believe that we, now more than at any other time, need to understand the dictatorship syndrome. The victims of dictatorship worldwide outnumber those struck down by any disease.

Once in New York, I resumed work. The chapters were translated one by one and sent on to Charles who made most valuable comments on the text, as did the publisher at Haus, Harry Hall.

Dear reader, you now have my book in your hands. I hope you like it.

1

The syndrome

I was a boy of ten when the 1967 war between Egypt and Israel broke out. Gamal Abdel Nasser (1918–1970) was in sole charge of Egypt and took oppressive and violent measures against any and every person who put up opposition to him. Notwithstanding his authoritarianism, Nasser had adopted revolutionary socialist policies,[1] had nationalised the large corporations and had seized the holdings of the large landowners and distributed them to the peasants. For the first time, the millions of poor people had been given the opportunity of free education, health insurance, jobs in the civil service and affordable housing. All of this ultimately resulted in Nasser gaining the sort of sweeping popularity rarely enjoyed by any Egyptian leader.[2]

At that time, the Egyptian people were buffered from what was going on in the world because the Nasserite propaganda machine shaped public opinion in Egypt in accordance with instructions from the security apparatus. Foreign radio stations, such as the BBC and the Voice of America, were subjected to continuous scrambling, and the authorities warned citizens against listening to them as they "broadcast lies and anti-revolutionary propaganda".[3] Nasser thought of himself as a world leader responsible for standing up to colonialism globally, and in line with his conception of Arab nationalism he had declared a union between Egypt and Syria in 1958. However, the overbearing behaviour of the Egyptian top brass caused Syria to revolt and secede from the union in September 1961. Then, in 1962, Nasser sent the Egyptian army to Yemen to support the Republicans against the Royalists and became bogged down in an absurd war that led to the deaths of thousands of soldiers and the exhaustion of the most efficient fighting units of the army. This whole debacle was kept hidden from the public in Egypt, and the Nasserite information machine still managed to convince us that our national army was the greatest fighting force in the Middle East and that one day it would crush the Israeli army within a few short hours and throw Israel into the sea as it liberated Palestine once and for all.

In May 1967, relations between Israel and Syria became tense. Nasser issued orders to amass huge military forces in the East of the country and announced the activation of the Joint Defence Agreement he had signed with Syria.[4] He demanded that the United Nations withdraw its emergency forces from the Egyptian border, and then suddenly decreed that Israeli ships would not be allowed to sail through the Gulf of Aqaba. It all looked as if Nasser were gunning for a war with Israel. We Egyptians had not the slightest doubt that we would defeat Israel – so much so that many people started speaking about the spoils Egypt would take after the victory.

Back then, I lived with my family in Garden City, an elegant district of Cairo in which the residents were mostly the great landowners or businessmen who had been the most adversely affected by the new socialist laws. In spite of that, they all gave enthusiastic support to their country in the war. Pursuant to the regulations issued by the civil defence authorities, residents covered their windows with black-out paint to prevent enemy aircraft being able to target them. Brick roadblocks were thrown up and sandbags placed in front of the entrances to buildings in order to protect them from the anticipated bomb shrapnel. I can still remember the slogans written on the enormous cloth banners, which the Cairo Governorate strung up in the street: "If you sail up the Gulf, we'll throw you to the wolf!" and "We'll be drinking our tea in Tel-Aviv by the sea."

My father, Abbas Al Aswany, was a famous socialist writer and lawyer, and he was among those most sharply opposed to Nasser. Although he was in agreement with all of the socialist measures that Nasser had implemented, he believed that they would not last long, because achievements had no value if not accompanied by freedom (his predictions in fact did come true, as Nasser's achievements all crumbled like a house of cards almost as soon as he died[5]). I can still remember a sentence that my father never tired of repeating: "All the socialist achievements are worth absolutely nothing if even a single person's dignity is impugned."

The war with Israel broke out on the morning of 5 June 1967, and everyone was consumed by nationalist fervour – including my father, who described his stance to me in conversation, "I have not stopped opposing the dictator Gamal Abdel Nasser, but today, as Egypt is waging war, I am supporting Egypt."

We all felt so strongly that everybody had to play a part

in the battle, even us children, that I set up a small 'information clearing house' on our balcony. Our neighbours in the building opposite were an Italian family consisting of a grandmother (Marta), her son, his wife and their children. I loved 'Auntie Marta' and used to chat away with her in French as she watered the mass of flowers on her balcony. On the morning the war broke out, Auntie Marta smiled and greeted me sweetly. She told me how much she loved Egypt and hoped that we would defeat Israel. I used to translate for her the military communiqués we heard broadcast over the radio. I told her that we had downed 23 Israeli planes. A little while later, I informed her that the number had risen to 46, and then 87. When I informed her that we, according to the latest communiqué, had brought down 200 Israeli planes, she shook her head and said, with some emotion in her voice, "Listen, my boy. Your government is lying to you. I lived through the Second World War and it is impossible for so many planes to have been downed in one day."

Naturally, I was irritated by this attitude, and so I stopped translating the military communiqués for Auntie Marta. The Nasserite propaganda machine succeeded in convincing us that we had inflicted a crushing defeat on Israel. Our nation had the wool pulled over its eyes for two whole days, but on the third day Egyptians woke up to the news that Egypt had agreed a ceasefire and had submitted a complaint to the United Nations over Israel having attacked the Egyptian army as it was withdrawing from Sinai. This horrible shock was tantamount to an earthquake for the Egyptian mindset, and I don't think we have recovered from it to this day.

On 9 June, the fifth day of the war, the magnitude of
the disaster became clear. Israel had destroyed the Egyptian air force in the first hours of the war and had gone on
to occupy Sinai, the West Bank, Gaza, the Golan Heights
and East Jerusalem. This was a humiliating defeat in
Egypt's history,[6] and I can still remember how my father's
friends gathered in our building, unable to believe what
had happened, with some of them even bursting into tears
like children. In the middle of this catastrophe, the state
television announced that our leader, Nasser, was going
to address the nation. My father was in an awful psychological state and was angrier than ever at Nasser who, in
addition to being a tyrant, had now brought disaster and
shame upon Egypt. That evening, Nasser appeared on the
television looking forlorn and exhausted and announced
that Egypt had been the victim of a great colonialist conspiracy, that the colonialist powers considered him to be
their enemy and that they did not realise that the whole
Arab nation was inimical to them. He then confirmed that
he was "prepared to bear the whole responsibility for the
setback" (as he euphemistically referred to the defeat) and
went on to state that he had taken a decision that he hoped
Egyptians would support, which was that he was going to
resign from his position and would thereafter serve Egypt
as an ordinary soldier. The moment he finished making
his speech, millions of people rushed out onto the streets
all over Egypt, calling for him to stay in power. I sat next
to my father as we watched Nasser on the television, and
when he heard the shouts of the throngs of people on the
street calling for Nasser to stay on, my father could take it
no more. He took me with him in the car and drove around

the streets amid the demonstrations, and then he suddenly stopped the car and asked one of the demonstrators, "Why are you out here demonstrating?"

The man replied, "We don't want Nasser to go."

My father asked him, "You do know that Israel has defeated us and occupied our land?"

"Yes, I know that."

"Nasser is the one who brought about this defeat, so he has to go."

At this point, the man looked at my father with something akin to panic and said, "But sir, if Nasser goes, who's going to hold us all together?"

"Do we need someone to hold us together? Can't we do that by ourselves?" My father shouted angrily, and then drove away from the man.

Two days after the mass demonstrations, Nasser announced that he was submitting to the will of the masses and withdrawing his resignation. He was in power for three years more, until he died.

To this day, Nasser's abdication threat arouses differences of opinion among historians. Opponents of Nasser believe that the demonstrations calling for him to stay were organised by the security apparatus, and those who support Nasser consider the demonstrations to have been the natural reaction of the masses. As far as I saw with my own eyes, people thronged out onto the streets without being directed by anyone, and I will never forget the expression of panic on the face of that man, who had no idea how the country could remain united if Nasser were to give up power.

When I was an adult, I recalled that conversation between

my father and the demonstrator, and I had a deeper understanding of it than when I was a child. It seemed to me that the view of that demonstrator (and of the millions like him) was odd, almost unfathomable. It goes without saying: if individuals are responsible for their own mistakes, how much more so a leader who causes such a terrible defeat for his country? How could Egyptians not hold him accountable and instead call for him to stay in his post? I compared this strange state of mind to what happened in Britain on 8 May 1945 when Winston Churchill announced the surrender of Germany in the Second World War. The British viewed Churchill as their hero, but in the first elections after the end of the war in Europe (in July 1945) they did not give their votes to him, and he was not re-elected as prime minister. The British people realised that the man who was best able to lead them in war was not necessarily the one to lead them in peacetime, and they elected a new prime minister who would bring new thinking to the process of rebuilding post-war Britain.

Why did the Egyptians want to hold on to their defeated leader, whereas the British decided to replace their victorious leader? The facile answer to this question is to say that Islam, the religion of the majority of Egyptians, is so out of step with democracy that it makes Muslims more receptive to authoritarianism. However, this simplistic argument falls apart immediately when we recall that dictatorships have been in place in Argentina, Italy, Spain, Germany, Portugal, Chile and many other non-Muslim countries. If religion is not the reason, then why did the Egyptians behave differently to the British? Why did Churchill's victory not sway the British to re-elect him, and why were the Egyptians more concerned about Nasser staying in office than about their defeat and the occupation of their country?

The question kept repeating itself in my mind, and I could find no convincing answer for it until I came across Étienne de La Boétie. He was a sixteenth-century French philosopher who died young, leaving behind a short essay that was published posthumously: *The Discourse of Voluntary Servitude*.[7] In this essay, he presented the following notions.

First: liberty as the natural disposition of humankind. La Boétie states that animals are born free and that their natural disposition impels them to defend their freedom with all the power they possess. We cannot dispossess an animal of its freedom without causing it pain. Every animal fights valiantly to defend its freedom, and not only do most animals prefer death to servitude but the elephant, for example, will keep fighting the hunter, and when it feels that it is on the verge of defeat resorts to a last stratagem whereby it dashes its jaws against the trees and breaks off its tusks, as its last effort to buy off the hunter in the hope that the sacrifice of its tusks will serve as a ransom for its liberty. Any animal will go this far to conserve its liberty. Humankind is born free like the animals, except that we sometimes give up our freedom willingly and accept a submissive life under the rule of a tyrant.

Second: the tyrant is an individual. La Boétie states that a tyrant is no more than an individual who could scarcely command the obedience of an entire people if the people did not grant him their obedience by their own consent. Hence a dictatorship – a country ruled by a head of state with complete power over the policies of state, the armed forces and security agencies, who crushes political opposition and eliminates forms of dissent – does not come about by the will of the tyrant alone but is a human relationship in which two parties are necessary: the tyrant who decides to subjugate a people and a people who have accepted such subjugation.

Third: voluntary servitude. The moment a population waives certain freedoms and submits, by conquest or deception, to the will of one individual, that individual becomes a dictator.* This is where we see the argument between natural disposition and custom: the natural disposition that impels a person to defend their liberty (as with an animal) and the custom that people acquire through long submission to the will of a tyrant. Custom gets the better of natural disposition, and generations of people arise who are completely habituated to the idea of authoritarianism, as they know nothing else. This acclimatisation to authoritarianism is likened by La Boétie to a horse that resists being trained and refuses its rider until it finally submits and not only gives itself over to guidance but starts to prance proudly beneath the saddle and bit, both of which are symbols of its servitude. This is similar to the generations who grow up under the rule of a dictator, who neither understand the meaning of liberty nor feel the need for it – because a person, as La Boétie states, does not miss something they have never possessed. However, there are

---

* Editor's note: Dictatorship is a condition that, so far in our history, has related only to men. While many women have been accused of behaving in a dictatorial fashion – such as Elena Ceaușescu, Mirjana Marković and Sajida Khairallah Talfah – no woman has been definitively labelled a dictator. As such, this book refers to dictators throughout as 'he'.

fortunately some individuals who long for liberty because, even if they have never been blessed with it, they are still capable of imagining it, and it is these individuals who will reject servitude and strive to free themselves.

After the death of Nasser, the great Egyptian writer Tawfiq al-Hakim wrote a book entitled *The Return of Consciousness* (1974)[8] in which he condemned himself for having supported Nasser and for having ignored the many clear signs that showed that the decisions taken by Nasser were erroneous, were emotionally driven and had brought about the catastrophes from which Egyptians are still suffering to this day. Al-Hakim likened himself to a man who has lost his consciousness to the charismatic tyranny of Nasser. Al-Hakim may well have been describing the situation of millions of Egyptians when he wrote:

[Nasser] put such a spell on us that we did not even realise we had become bewitched. Perhaps it was his special magic, as they say, or perhaps it was the dream itself which gave us such hopes and promises. Or maybe it was even more that wonderful image of revolutionary achievements which he wove for us and which turned us into instruments of that far-reaching propaganda with all its drums, pipes, anthems, songs and films and enabled us to see ourselves as a great industrialised state which was leading the developing world in agricultural reform and was the leading force in the Middle East. It was the face of that worshipped leader which filled the television screens, which peered down on us from tents erected for political rallies and in assembly halls and as he orated for hours on end, telling us how we had been and what we had now become with no space for discussion or review, no space for comment or correction. All we could do was believe and clap until our hands were raw.[9]

For the first time I could find a convincing explanation for the way Egyptians clung on to their defeated leader. People who submit to a dictator lose their yearning for liberty and behave in the manner of the sick who seem to be bewitched, hypnotised or unconscious. The Egyptians were struck down with the plague of submission to a dictator and they clung to him after he had brought about defeat, whereas the British enjoyed the sort of psychological wellbeing that made them elect a prime minister other than Churchill, the man who had led them to victory. It might be suggested that people ruled by a dictator can be compared to those suffering from a mental illness: not only do they not need liberty or strive for it but they also cannot imagine a life without the dictator whom they protect and whose will they embody. Medicine recognises a disease to be something that afflicts people and prevents them from fulfilling themselves in their personal and professional lives. Submission to a dictator is thus a disease that afflicts individuals and peoples, like the demonstrator I saw who was panic-stricken over the resignation of Nasser. On the other hand, studies confirm that, no matter how different their culture, social background or educational level, all tyrants – once they are in power – are made of the same stuff.[10] Muammar Gaddafi, Saddam Hussein, Gamal Abdel Nasser, Jean-Bédel Bokassa, Adolf Hitler, Benito Mussolini, Francisco Franco and António de Oliveira Salazar, to mention but a few, were tyrants who emerged in various countries and under different circumstances, but once in power they all behaved and thought similarly. In a paper entitled "The Psychology of Tyrants", Dr Azzam Amin states that all tyrants suffer from "narcissism and megalomania ... paranoia and sadism".[11]

Dictatorship thus represents the sick relationship between a ruler and a people, and the symptoms of a dictatorship manifest through all the instruments of authoritarianism in a similar fashion. The presentation of various symptoms repeated in a similar mode makes this illness, in the language of medicine, a *syndrome*. For how long will our world continue to suffer from the dictatorship syndrome?

The discussion of dictatorship in the United States and Western Europe has acquired an exotic dimension, as Western Europe has rarely known dictatorship since the Second World War. When it comes to Africa, Asia, the Middle East and Latin America, dictatorship is not an exotic narrative but a painful reality with which millions of people have to contend. Research published in 2017 by the freedom and democracy watchdog organisation Freedom House, using the Universal Declaration of Human Rights as its benchmark, shows that there are only 87 free countries out of the 195 states covered by the study, and that there are 49 'not free' and 59 'partially free' countries. Of the 7.4 billion people on earth, only 39 per cent enjoy full freedom, 36 per cent are deprived of freedom and 25 per cent live in partial freedom.[12] Thus there are billions of people who live under authoritarian regimes, with all that term entails regarding the violation of freedoms, the abuse of human rights, arrest, torture and extrajudicial killings, corruption, inefficiency, poverty, ignorance, infectious disease and social injustice.

Dictatorship is a disease that represents a danger to humanity and must be dealt with. The first step in the treatment of any disease is to study its causes, the circumstances of its emergence and the symptoms and complications it gives rise to in both the people and the dictator. This is what we will do in this book.

2

Symptoms of the dictatorship syndrome

Amr had been my friend since childhood. I was three years older than him and he used to treat me like his big brother, asking me for advice on issues in his life. His dream was to become a famous journalist. I can still remember how happy he was at getting high-enough marks in his final exams to be admitted to the media college, and again when he graduated and found a placement as an intern at a major state-run newspaper. Amr started out in the arts and culture section, where his task was to follow the news about celebrities in the film and music industries.

He had already been working there for a number of months when he came to see me in a state of agitation and said, "I've found out that the head of the arts and culture department is corrupt."

"How do you know that?"

"He gets monthly backhanders from movie stars to give them publicity."

"What proof do you have?"

"I noticed that he only publishes positive pieces on certain stars and refuses to allow anything to get into print regarding certain others. Last week he sent me to do an interview with a pop star, and as I was leaving she handed me an envelope and asked me to pass it on to my boss. When I gave him the envelope, he opened it, counted the money and then peeled off a hundred-pound note for me."

"What did you do?"

"I refused to take it, and requested a transfer to another department."

I was full of admiration for Amr's stance. He was just an intern whom the newspaper could dismiss at any moment, but in spite of that he would not go against his conscience. Amr's request was granted, and he was transferred to the politics desk. His new task was to follow what was going on in parliament, news about ministers and any other government officials – excluding the president of the republic, as there was a special section in the newspaper dedicated to him. A few months passed with Amr rarely coming to visit me, and I simply ascribed that to his being too busy with his work – until one evening, when he came to see me looking exhausted and troubled. I asked him how he was, and with a downcast smile he replied, "I have an enormous problem."

"I hope it's nothing too awful."

"I've been asked to cover the referendum being held by President Mubarak tomorrow to reconfirm his presidency."

"So what's the problem?"

"I'm sure you're aware that no one goes to vote in these referendums except for a small number of people paid to do so by the ruling party and bussed in to vote for the president."

"I may have heard something of the sort."

"I'm being asked to write about how the citizens have thronged to the polling stations to renew their support for the president, and I'll have to resort to using old archival images and publishing them as if they were taken now."

"And who's asking you to do that?"

"No one has asked me in so many words, but my colleagues in the politics section keep telling me that if I don't cover the referendum in this manner I'll never have a permanent position at the newspaper."

I warned Amr against doing as his colleagues were advising him. I told him it would be a dishonourable act, and that getting a permanent position at the newspaper was not worth his becoming a hypocrite and a liar. I went on at him until he was completely convinced and told me enthusiastically, "I shall write the truth. I shall not lie, so let them do their worst."

As he was leaving, I hugged him and my respect for him grew. It is easy to talk about principles, but it can be hugely costly to defend them. But two days later, when I read Amr's coverage of the referendum, I was greatly taken aback. The headline read "Unprecedented popular support for President Mubarak", and indeed the article was illustrated by old photographs showing masses of people standing in long queues outside the polling stations. Amr had written a whole page of lies, concluding something along the lines of, "Egyptians turned out as one to renew their loyalty to the great leader Mubarak whom God has sent to bring about our renaissance and to put Egypt in its rightful place at the forefront of nations."

I was furious and tried to telephone Amr at home and at work, but he kept coming up with excuses not to talk to me. It was clear that he did not wish to hear what I had to say.

My friendship with Amr came to an end that day, but he shot up like a star in the newspaper's firmament and he is now the editor-in-chief of one of the largest weeklies as well as being the director general of one of the largest online news sites in Egypt. Amr's predicament is not exceptional. In fact, it is the first rule of getting a promotion or a new position in any dictatorial state. In Egypt you will never be able to get a job in the civil service without the authorisation of the security apparatus, which categorises citizens as four types: supporter, collaborator, opponent and protestor. A regime supporter will always get priority when it comes to senior positions. Ministers in Egypt are never chosen for their fitness for purpose, but primarily because they support the regime; consequently, their first concern is to demonstrate their loyalty in order to keep themselves in the job. Senior officials support everything the president says, whether he is right or spouting nonsense. Should any official object to what the president says, appear to query his words or simply not show enough enthusiastic support, the consequence will be dismissal.

When swine flu was spreading around the world, instead of taking preventative measures President Hosni Mubarak (1928–2020) suddenly issued a bizarre decree ordering the killing of every single pig in Egypt.[1] In the government at that time there were a number of ministers who were trained doctors and who knew that the president's decree was wrong, but not a single one of them dared to raise any objections. Officials rushed into action in order to please the president. Tens of thousands of pigs were kept by Egyptian Copts, and the whole affair descended into a farce. Workers in the provinces loaded pigs on to open trucks to be taken away to be slaughtered, but the unfortunate animals could sense the danger and scores of them started jumping off the trucks, causing traffic jams on the highways. In one province, matters came to the point where pigs were thrown alive into pits and covered with lime in order to please Mubarak.[2] This barbaric practice went on until international animal welfare societies threatened to take the Egyptian government to court.[3]

The year 2005 saw domestic and international pressure increase on Mubarak to institute some democratic reforms. However, he rejected any change to the constitution and declared that constitutions were not a game to be changed lightly. The state media picked up on this tune and started piping on about any change to the constitution being a notion promoted by traitors and agents in the pay of foreigners who wanted to see the downfall of the Egyptian state. The following day, Mubarak was making a televised visit to a provincial university and the chancellor of the university gave an impassioned speech welcoming the great leader Mubarak and heaping praise upon him for being such a towering intellectual. He went on to deride those who were suggesting that the constitution needed amending, accusing them of being traitors and agents of the American and Israeli secret services. Next came the turn of the president, and he gave a short speech in which he announced that he had, in fact, decided to effect some amendments to the constitution. There was silence for a moment, followed by warm applause. Then the university chancellor picked up the microphone and lauded the democratic sensitivity of the great leader, thanking him warmly for responding to the people's request for a change to the constitution. The university chancellor was an academic in charge of many lecturers and thousands of students, but he felt no embarrassment at enthusiastically supporting one opinion and then, less than an hour later, taking the opposite position in front of the millions of Egyptians watching his hypocrisy on television. In a dictatorship, the chancellor's change of tune was seen by everyone to be a necessary form of duty and consequently not a matter that would give rise to any feelings of embarrassment.[4]

I happen to know a few actors in Egypt, and in our private meetings they express rather acerbic criticism of the president of the republic, but the moment they are being interviewed on television they shower him with praise and do everything they can to display their loyalty to him. These movie stars consider it prudent to show such hypocritical loyalty to the president as a way to protect their artistic future; the police state could blacklist them at any moment. This all happens behind the scenes, and it takes no more than a telephone call from an intelligence officer to a producer or a cable channel for the actor who has fallen out of favour to find that they are out of work.

In schools, children receive early lessons in duplicity when they are given essay topics such as 'The Great Achievements of President Mubarak' or 'How has President Mubarak, in his Wisdom and Courage, Saved Egypt and Led Her to a Renaissance?' From a young age, children learn that what they see with their own eyes is one thing and what they have to write down is something completely different. There was an instance when a secondary school pupil called Alaa Farag broke these rules and wrote an essay that was deemed critical of the president of the republic.[5] And what happened?

The teacher stopped marking her exam paper and contacted the authorities. The young girl was arrested along with her father, and they were subjected to a lengthy interrogation. The minister of education decided to fail the young girl in all her subjects and to prevent her from taking her exams the following year. A public relations spokesperson for the Ministry of Education declared that they had discovered that she was the child of "a political deviant". President Mubarak used this incident to boost his flagging popularity and ordered the young girl and her father to be released. He even telephoned her afterwards to reassure her. Only then did the ministry fall in with the president's instructions. They allowed her to study for her exams the following year and restricted themselves to failing her in just one examination because of her "abhorrent" essay.

Every six years, Egyptians see the same scene on their televisions: the minister of the interior stands next to the president of the republic to read out the results of a referendum from the sheets of paper in front of him, finally declaring to the president that he has won the confidence of the Egyptian people by a figure that varies between 97 and 99 per cent. The minister congratulates the president, who appears moved. E-mails congratulating the president flood in from officials all across the country, while the media broadcast patriotic songs all day long and the security services mobilise their followers in large rallies to laud the president for his success. Everyone, including the president, knows that the results of the referendum are a total fiction, but there is a general agreement to accept the lie. The president demonstrates his delight at the results, and officials make public shows of congratulating him.

The huge gap between reality and what appears on our television screens is not restricted to presidential affairs. The hypocrisy surrounding the dictator quickly spreads its contagion into every section of society and underscores the contradiction between word and deed, between the hypothetical and the feasible, between form and content. Every citizen understands that not everything that takes place can be spoken about, and that not everything that is spoken about is necessarily what is taking place. The moment that the young journalist, Amr, decided to write false coverage of the referendum was not just a moment of weakness when he strayed from his principles but a real epiphany. It was the moment when Amr grasped that society is governed by robust yet invisible rules that differ from those officially authorised. Amr found himself face to face with a giant apparatus; he could either give in to it, advancing along its limited path, or attempt to resist it and end up crushed. Had he refused to write a false report about the referendum, the newspaper would have found hundreds of other interns willing to lie. Amr would have lost his job on the spot and would have joined a small number of 'untouchables', designated by the dictatorship to spend the rest of their lives protesting bitterly and to no avail while society carries on promoting those willing to be complicit and dance to the piper's tune.

If you are Egyptian, there is no way of avoiding Amr's experience. If you are a doctor, you will find colleagues in the health service reluctant to provide free treatment to the sick and instead directing them to their private clinics. If you are an engineer, you will find your colleagues and your boss taking backhanders in order to overlook violations of building regulations. If you are a police officer, you will be well aware that the law is only applied to the person in the street and that if you try to apply it to important people, the movers and shakers or the rich, harsh consequences will be applied to you. If you are a law student, you will understand that, no matter how good a student you are, you will never become a member of the lawyers' union because the places are reserved for the children of judges or high-ranking officials. If you are a medical student, you will know that you will never get a job teaching medicine, because the positions are all reserved for the children of professors or those in positions of influence. If you are a woman, you will understand that society only respects you for the way you look, no matter what you might do in your private life; do what you wish, enjoy your sex life, but keep your hijab on and your hymen intact and you will gain everyone's respect as well as a groom who considers your virginity the only criterion of virtue. In a dictatorship, society lives in an acute and comprehensive state of duality. It is impossible for people to accept all the lies in the public domain and then show some sense of devotion to the truth in their own affairs and at home. In a dictatorship, there is always a contradiction between what is announced and the truth, between the hypothetical and the practical, between words and deeds. Nothing in an authoritarian society resembles the essence of its appearance. Hypocrisy in the political domain gradually turns into hypocrisy across all domains, and corruption goes beyond concept and into practice. Words take on different meanings and give a veneer of positivity to aberrations. Hypocrisy becomes propriety, cheating in exams becomes 'help', cowardice becomes wisdom and bribes become acts of cleverness. The worst thing that a dictatorship does is to destroy all rules of fairness in society, so that actions do not necessarily lead to logical consequences. Speaking the truth does not necessarily lead to respect for those who do so, and lying does not necessarily bring about contempt towards those who lie. Breaking the law does not necessarily lead to any sanction, and behaving according to the law does not necessarily keep one out of trouble. Intelligence, learning and serious work are not necessarily the paths that lead to success and promotion.

In many countries around the world, football is the popular game of choice, but my experience of football supporters in Egypt prompts me to state that their obsession with the game is not simply due to it being an enjoyable spectator sport. They enjoy it because its rules are just and transparent. Egyptians, downtrodden and despairing of ever seeing justice realised, regard football as a sort of parallel universe in which justice is seen to be done and in which 22 players are equal in face of the rules, which are applied by the referee and the line judges in a clear and transparent way in front of millions of spectators. In addition to the enjoyment that Egyptian fans derive from the game, the real sense of fairness that it presents over 90 minutes compensates them for the injustice they experience in their daily lives. In a dictatorship, the rot is not limited to individuals but ends up infecting the ethical system of society. One ends up with three options: to become corrupt, to isolate oneself or to emigrate.

Citizens of Western democracies, whose basic needs are satisfied and who enjoy the protection of the law, look on with shock and confusion at the tens of thousands of illegal migrants who leave their homelands, homes, relatives and friends and crowd onto boats making the dangerous trip across the Mediterranean, where they must confront the balance of risk between dying and surviving. What drives these desperate people to risk their lives is not just poverty but despair at ever seeing fairness reign in their countries. People can put up with poverty if they feel that there are fair rules for them to rely on. The poor in the democratic states of the West do not risk their lives trying to migrate because they know that, as difficult as it is to haul themselves out of poverty, it can be done. On the other hand, when you grow up poor in a dictatorship, you quickly learn that a place at the top, along with a life of ease and financial comfort, is a privilege reserved for the lucky few, and that no matter how much you try you will never be able to raise yourself out of the social abyss. You then realise that the only thing left to do is to flee, at any price.

Egyptians call the boats carrying these migrants "death ships".[6] When one of these death ships sank off the Egyptian coast, the migrants were rescued and one of them was interviewed on television. The journalist asked him, "What are you planning to do now that you have been saved from drowning?"

The young man gave the simple answer, "I'm going to try again."

The journalist was taken aback, and asked him, "Aren't you afraid of dying?"

And the young man responded, "If I manage to make it abroad there is a chance that I will be able to live, but in Egypt I am already dead."

3

The emergence of the good citizen

An oft-shared (though misrepresented) story describes an experiment carried out by a number of scientists. Five monkeys were placed in a large cage. A ladder was then put in the middle of the cage and a bunch of bananas placed on top of it. Whenever one monkey attempted to climb up the ladder to eat the bananas, the whole group was soaked with cold water. After some time, the monkeys came to grasp that being soaked was connected to any attempt to eat the bananas, and not only did they refrain from going after the fruit but they started to beat up any monkey who tried to do so. They all ended up sitting in the cage without attempting to climb the ladder for the bananas. At that point, the scientists took one of the monkeys out of the cage and replaced him with a new one who had no idea of the situation. The first thing the new monkey did was climb up the ladder for the bananas. The rest of the group set upon him and started hitting him, so he gave up the attempt. The scientists continued replacing one monkey at a time, with the same result. The moment a new monkey tried to climb after the bananas, the others in the group started hitting him to stop him from doing so. Finally, there were five new monkeys in the cage, none of whom had undergone the soaking punishment, but none of whom tried to climb up the ladder for the bananas or allowed any other monkey to do so. Though this experiment did not actually occur, the fact that the idea of it has spread so widely suggests that its representation of human relationships is a powerful one. In particular, the story elucidates an important aspect of the relationship between a dictator and the people.

The Iraqi dictator Saddam Hussein (1937–2006) once made a visit to a school as part of his endeavour to show himself as the compassionate ruler of all his people, little children included. He was inspecting the children and chatting with them when he came to one little boy. The dictator placed his hand on the boy's head and asked him, "Do you know who I am, little boy?"

The child answered naively, "Yes. I've seen you on the television and when my father sees you he spits at the screen."[1]

Thereupon Saddam Hussein's guards made the school give them the boy's address. They arrested his father, and two days later the man was dead from the severity of the torture to which he was subjected. The family was contacted and instructed to go and retrieve his body.[2]

On 25 July 1992, Saddam Hussein ordered the arrest of 38 Baghdad market traders, who were all tried and executed on that very day. The charge against these poor men was simply that they had been selling commodities for a price higher than that set by the state. Saddam Hussein also gave orders for dissidents' arms and legs to be broken and their tongues to be cut out, while Jean-Bédel Bokassa (1921–1996), the dictator of the Central African Republic, reportedly killed five children by smashing their skulls with his walking stick – among many other gruesome acts of violence.[3] Muammar Gaddafi (1942–2011), the Libyan dictator, used to order the execution of his adversaries in a football stadium as a form of public entertainment. In Egyptian prisons during the time of Gamal Abdel Nasser, detainees were subjected to degrading torture with electric shocks and then made to chant slogans in praise of the dictator. The same methods are used by the officers of Bashar al-Assad (b. 1965) in Syria, where, after being tortured, detainees are made to perform the Islamic prayer in Assad's name, rather than God's.[4] Francisco Macías Nguema (1924–1979), the dictator of Equatorial Guinea, rounded up 150 of his opponents on Christmas Eve 1975 and had them transported to a stadium in Malabo, where soldiers dressed as Father Christmas opened fire and killed them all as loudspeakers blared out Mary Hopkin's famous song "Those Were the Days".[5]

One can easily find copious examples of the unbelievable brutality of dictators, and this leads us to ask: do dictators need to commit these atrocious crimes in order to stay in power? Why do they exhibit such devotion to oppression and humiliation? Do they have to kill all those thousands of people in order to maintain their positions? We might understand it when a dictator orders the execution of officers who have been plotting a military coup against him, but history teaches us that most of the victims of a dictator represent no direct threat to his authority. So why torture and kill them? The answer might be that unfettered authority gives rise to brutality in a dictator who is so plagued by an exaggerated vision of self-worth that he cannot countenance the existence of anyone who either opposes him or simply does not support him enthusiastically enough. This is undoubtedly the case, but we may gain a deeper under-standing if we think back to the story of the monkeys.

When one monkey attempted to eat the bananas, not only was he punished but the whole group was punished by being soaked with cold water. The aim was to create an atmosphere of fear among the monkeys and to make them aware that they would all be subjected to punishment even if they were not the ones doing wrong. The result was that the monkeys would beat up any individual who attempted to eat the bananas. The monkeys were stopped from eating the bananas by a barrier of fear.

The creation of just such a barrier of fear is the aim of all dictators in their practice of oppression, and this can only be achieved by applying the foulest methods of abuse to any opponents. Once a dictator has succeeded in creating this barrier of fear, the exemplar of the 'good citizen' starts to appear in society. They are the ordinary person on the street whose whole world is centred on their small family and their job. They will always opt for stability over the uncer-tainty caused by attempts at political change. They prefer to carry on with the normal course of their life, no matter how much injustice and unfairness they suffer. This good citizen lives in despair and fear: despair that it will ever be possible to bring about justice and fear of the consequences of any attempt to do so. This type of person, who generally forms the majority in an authoritarian society, has been accurately described by Étienne de La Boétie in terms of their robust and chronic obedience. This good citizen has grown up in the penumbra of authoritarianism; it is their familiar world and they no longer yearn for freedom, for, as La Boétie puts it, a person cannot long for something of which they have no notion. They have no interest in anything outside the framework of the requirements of their daily life. They have come to understand that everything that takes place in their country is decreed solely by the ruler, and that if they tried to play some role in public affairs it would change nothing and they would only be bringing catastrophe upon themselves – arrest, torture and death.

This good citizen thus withdraws completely from the public arena except for the usual hypocritical lip service they are obliged to pay from time to time in order to keep their job, to keep themselves above suspicion and to confirm their loyalty to the ruler. The good citizen creates their own safe microworld in total isolation from everything going on outside it, and they are completely uninterested in anything except earning enough to bring up their children. Their sense of belonging is restricted to their spouse and children. They will give greater priority to tracking down a drug to increase their sexual potency than to the drafting of a new constitution for their country, just as to secure an employment contract in the Gulf for their son is more important than securing free and fair elections. Election day for them is just a holiday from work that they can spend with their family, and they only go to cast their vote in one set of circumstances: if they and the other workers have been ordered by their manager to do so to assure the president's continued term in power. The good citizen casts a jaded glance at those people who are struggling to bring about freedom, considering them at worst agents of foreign powers or at best misguided idiots. The good citizen simply cannot imagine that a person with any common sense would endanger their professional future or risk imprisonment and torture for the sake of hazy concepts such as democracy and freedom.

On 25 January 2011, Egyptians rose up to try to bring down the dictator Hosni Mubarak. It is estimated that the revolutionaries made up only about 20 per cent of the population – 20 million out of 90 million Egyptians. During the first days of the revolution, some of them held a meeting in the house of a sympathiser. When they felt hungry, they went out into the street to buy some sandwiches and then sat in a nearby café to have some tea. It was a run-of-the-mill place in a poor district of Cairo. The moment these young people sat down, the police burst in. In such circumstances, we would have expected the police to be hostile to the revolutionaries, but the opposite happened. The police protected them from the poverty-stricken customers of the café who, the moment they realised that the young people belonged to the revolution, started accusing them of treachery and tried to attack them. A police officer rounded up the youths and drove them off to the police station for their own safety. One of these young people had had in his pocket a piece of paper detailing the names of the leaders of the revolutionary movement he belonged to. He had surreptitiously torn it into little pieces and dropped them on the floor of the café to prevent the names falling into the wrong hands. Once at the police station, the officer started questioning the youths. A short while later, one of the customers from the café arrived, breathless, at the police station and gave the officer the scraps of paper that the young man had torn up, saying, "Officer, I saw this traitor tearing up a piece of paper, so I collected the bits from the floor and have come to hand them over to you."

This was the magnitude of the resentment felt by this man, along with other customers in the café, towards the revolution that had come about to defend their dignity and freedom.[6]

The good citizen neither understands nor wants revolution. They keep a wary eye on it and are the first to believe counter-revolutionary propaganda accusing revolutionaries of treachery and of working for foreign interests. In fact, they have a deep hatred of revolution, firstly because they have lost hope of justice ever being brought about or any change taking place that is not wanted by the leader, and secondly because the actions of the brave and heroic revolutionaries make them feel ashamed of themselves. They have become completely docile, having spent their life obeying and kowtowing to authority, and they feel a sense of unease at the thought of people attempting to resist authority and demand their rights. The bravery of the revolutionaries reveals them to themselves by making them see that what they previously considered to be their prudent behaviour is in fact no more than grotesque cowardice, and that their acquiescence to injustice is neither inevitable nor palatable.

The good citizen hopes that the revolutionaries will face harsh retribution – which will fulfil their prophecy that cowardly insularity is the best plan of action. They hate revolution because it is an attack on their microworld and it represents an obstacle to their own plans, to which they have devoted their life – earning a living and bringing up their children. The good citizen can never accept the notion that revolution, with all its demonstrations and disturbances, may well create difficulties for them today but will afford them their full rights in the near future. They will not be budged or held back for even a day from realising their plans, and furthermore the notion of struggling for the sake of freedom only arouses their cynicism, or, in the best of cases, remains an abstract expression devoid of any real meaning that might affect their senses or their mind.

Hence, it is natural that the good citizen is completely incapable of taking part in the sort of teamwork that is based on the realisation of any common interest. The good citizen has no common interest, only that of themselves and their family. Anyone who lives in Egypt will notice that most of the residents of the building they live in are prepared to splash out mindlessly on renovating their own flats but at the same time do everything they can to wriggle out of contributing towards the costs of repairing the lift or having a water pump installed. They will notice that their neighbours are meticulous when it comes to the cleanliness of their own apartments but are completely uninterested in the common areas of the building; they go mad if they see a speck of dust on their dining tables, but they can just as easily dump their rubbish in the building's light well or on the stairwell a little distance from their own flats. The good citizen has absolutely no interest in what takes place outside their own home and family and will not spend a pound beyond their small circle, basing this approach on the common Egyptian adage 'charity begins at home' – which allows them to carry out all sorts of self-interested ruses and schemes without feeling an iota of guilt.

The good citizen in Egypt only feels themselves to be a part of the two domains of football and religion. In football they find everything that is lacking in their daily life: fair and unified rules applied to everyone, transparency of decision-making, a meritocratic process. When it comes to religion, they understand it in a way that has no revolutionary meaning, in a way that has nothing to do with justice or resistance to injustice. Religion, as far as they are concerned, is a book of procedures, like those of any large company, with steps for acquiring God's satisfaction such as praying, wearing the veil, giving alms and making the various types of pilgrimage if they are a Muslim or going to church on Sunday and donating money to the church if they are a Christian. This is how a good citizen assures themselves of God's satisfaction, and how they manage to come across as a pious person respected by all while at the same time assuring themselves of their fate in the hereafter. For them, the rituals of religion are regular payments to an endowment policy that, when they die, they can cash in as they enter paradise.

The good citizen can be found in any authoritarian system and, despite being a victim of the dictator, they most often feel respect and gratitude towards the ruler. Between 1932 and 1968, the dictator António de Oliveira Salazar (1889–1970) ruled Portugal with an iron fist and had thousands of Portuguese citizens arrested and tortured.[7] In 2007, decades after his death, an opinion poll for Portuguese state television on the greatest figure in Portuguese history showed Salazar in first place with 41 per cent of the viewers' votes.[8] Those who voted for Salazar stated that they considered his oppressive methods to have been no more than a mistake that could have been made by any ruler, and that furthermore they believed Salazar had saved Portugal and had been a first-rate statesman who brought about security, stability and economic wellbeing. Many of them also felt that Portugal was in dire need of a new Salazar.

This hankering for the era of authoritarianism will show itself in any public opinion poll held after the downfall of a dictator, for there are always some people who consider bloodthirsty dictators such as Joseph Stalin (1878–1953), Muammar Gaddafi and Saddam Hussein to be great and matchless statesmen. In this regard we should note that after the downfall of Bokassa, a song came out praising him as the leader of the nation and father of the people,[9] and it achieved great success. The explanation for this odd phenomenon is that a large sector of the people had become exemplars of that good citizen who identifies with authoritarianism and hence cares not a whit about the rigging of elections or the monopolisation of power, and is indifferent to torture and killing provided it is not happening to their own children. The good citizen only sees the positive side of the dictator – security, a guaranteed job and a stable life under the wing of a paternalistic strongman who shields them from the ills of the world.

The good citizen and the dictator are two sides of the same coin. In the final analysis a dictator is just one man and his guards could arrest him at any moment, for no matter how strong his institutions of oppression, they cannot hold back a whole people when they decide to rise up. The emergence of the good citizen is one of the worst symptoms of dictatorship, and they are the primary culprits of a dictator's longevity in power, as well as of the length of time it takes for any revolution to be fomented against him and potentially also of the failure of any attempted revolution, should it come about.

4

The conspiracy theory

This is how they were depicted: a group of aged men, all dressed in black, with scowling, brooding faces and long beards. They uttered few words and spoke in whispers. At the appointed time, they filed into a gloomy candlelit basement where they met to decide upon the fate of the whole world.

They were the Elders of Zion, a group of evil men in an avid quest for power, money and blood. They wrote down their malevolent designs with their own hands in 24 documents in which they detail how to use mendacity, fraud, perversion and gambling to overturn Christian morality and to control the gentiles and herd them like cattle. The Elders of Zion themselves took the minutes of this meeting:

> For the sake of victory, we must keep to the programme of violence and make-believe. (Protocol, No. 1)

> By want and the envy and hatred which it engenders we shall move the mobs and with their hands we shall wipe out all those who hinder us on our way. (Protocol, No. 3)

> ...Thereby [we will] throw all the *goyim* [gentiles] into the ranks of the proletariat. Then the *goyim* will bow down before us, if for no other reason but to gain the right to exist. (Protocol, No. 6)[1]

Anyone who reads *The Protocols of the Learned Elders of Zion* will realise straight away not only that it is a fabrication but also that the person who authored the work lacked the elementary dramatic writing skills that demand that every protagonist, no matter how dastardly, should commit their evil actions according to some sort of overarching logic. However, the Elders of Zion do just the opposite, strangely incriminating themselves as they inform the reader of the extent of their sinister criminal designs.

Researchers have long concluded that this work is a forgery[2] likely written by Matvei Vasilyevich Golovinski, an operative of Tsar Nicholas II's secret police (the *Okhrana*), and first published in Russia in around 1905. The book's aim was to stoke anti-Semitic feeling. Despite being simplistic and pedestrian, the forgery was popular in pre-Nazi Germany and even more so once Adolf Hitler (1889–1945) was in power.[3] Hitler himself was so influenced by *The Protocols* that his speeches often seem to draw on its ideas, as for example in a 1933 speech:

> It is a small, rootless, international clique that is turning the people against each other, that does not want them to have peace ... It is the people who are at home both nowhere and everywhere, who do not have anywhere a [home] soil on which they have grown up, but who live in Berlin today, in Brussels tomorrow, Paris the day after

that, and then again in Prague or Vienna or London, and who feel at home everywhere. They are the only ones who can be addressed as international, because they conduct their business everywhere, but the people cannot follow them.[4]

Or in a speech from 1940:

A satanic power had taken hold of our whole nation who had gripped in their hand all the key positions of the spiritual and intellectual life, but also of the political and economic life, and who, from these key positions, monitored the whole nation ... [5]

For Hitler, the demonisation of the Jews was the first step towards the 'final solution', the Holocaust, which was to be one of the ugliest pages in the history of humankind, when the Nazis carried out the merciless annihilation of 6 million Jews. The Nazi regime eventually fell and its ideas all but died out, but the popularity of the forged and facile *The Protocols* did not wane.[6] In the Arab world, even today, you will often hear *The Protocols* mentioned in the Friday sermon in any mosque. I myself even witnessed, during a student competition at Cairo University in 1979, a 'general knowledge' question about *The Protocols* addressed to one of the competitors, with the quizmaster naturally convinced of the work's authenticity. With the spread of the extremist interpretation of Islam promulgated by the Wahhabis with the support of oil money, *The Protocols* has gained new significance among Islamist extremists as it enables them to view the Israel–Palestine conflict as a holy war to be waged against Jews by Muslims.[7]

The wide dissemination of such a shabby forgery shows how easy it is for a conspiracy theory to go viral. Without exception, every dictator who has seized power in the modern era has ridden the crest of a conspiracy theory. A conspiracy theory asserts that the events we experience do not happen spontaneously or naturally but are the result of a plot hatched in secret. This way of thinking is perfectly apt for a dictator, as he does not view himself as simply a president or prime minister but as a great leader who embodies his nation and turns the hopes and dreams of his people into reality. He presents himself as a strongman blessed by fate and uniquely capable of saving his nation from perdition and bringing about its rebirth and victory. A dictator, afflicted by megalomania, is incapable of imagining that he can do anything wrong. He is incapable of accepting any criticism and does not depend upon, despite enjoying, approval from other people. Nor can he admit that his opponents act according to any form of logic or sense of resolve; to his mind, opposition is irrational. Consequently, in his opinion, any opponents are no more than a group of traitors or agents funded by hostile intelligence bodies with the aim of sabotaging or bringing down the state.

The last moments before the downfall of any dictator are all surprisingly similar, confirming to us that all tyrants think in this way, no matter the country or culture they belong to. In the last press conference held by Hosni Mubarak before the revolution forced him from power, he insisted that the Kefaya movement (founded in 2004 and also known as the Egyptian Movement for Change) that instigated the protests against him was simply an organisation funded from abroad with the aim of holding Egypt down. Similar sentiments were expressed by the Romanian dictator Nicolae Ceauşescu (1918–1989), who accused the revolutionaries who had forced him from office of being Soviet and American agents at one and the same time![8] In the case of Muammar Gaddafi, the Libyan dictator, he appeared on television in his last days in power and hurled invective at the revolutionaries, saying, "I am the person who has made Libya what it is today. Who are you? You are traitors and agents of America and Israel."[9]

A conspiracy theory, so well-suited to the psychological makeup of a dictator, has always been an essential tool in any system of absolute rule. A dictator's pursuit of total control of the media reflects his deep disdain for his people and his belief that the people lack the ability to think for themselves. He believes that they need someone to help them think correctly, and this naturally increases the leader's own credibility. Moreover, a dictator's media machinery works tirelessly at cementing the notion of conspiracy in the minds of the masses.

A conspiracy theory shores up a dictator in a number of ways. First, a conspiracy theory ruins the image of the opposition and brings about its figurative assassination once and for all. The masses – bewitched by their leader's charisma and believing in the conspiracy theory – will resent, despise or even kill members of the opposition if they can, since in their eyes the opposition is made up of traitors and operatives carrying out a conspiracy against the nation. Indeed, on the street, supporters of Abdel Fattah el-Sisi (b. 1954), the present Egyptian dictator, find themselves compelled to beat up any of el-Sisi's adversaries[10] – many of whom are simply good young people and brave revolutionaries who have paid a crushing price to bring about democratic change. However, in the eyes of the dictator's followers, these people are traitors who ought to be 'finished off'. The same logic has been adopted by the supporters of the new 'tsar' of Russia, Vladimir Putin (b. 1952). His supporters organise well-attended demonstrations where they hold up photographs of members of the opposition, upon which the word 'traitor' is written in capital letters.[11]

Second, a conspiracy theory spreads a climate of fear among the people as they really are afraid that the great conspiracy might succeed and that their country will descend into chaos and civil war. Consequently, they cling ever more tightly to their leader as their protector. Notwithstanding his shortcomings, he remains the only person capable of foiling the conspiracy and holding the country and state together. He is their paternalistic shepherd, and they are his flock of children. He knows, better than anyone else, what is in their interest. He protects them; he alone can grasp the deep and precise meaning of events, and he makes the right decisions on their behalf. The more the notion of a conspiracy spreads, the more people unthinkingly follow the leader in their belief that he is the only one capable of protecting them from evil.

Third, a conspiracy theory prevents a dictator being held accountable for his mistakes or even his crimes. He can always ascribe any failure to the great conspiracy and the masses will cling to him even more, as he is the only one capable of challenging the conspirators. In 1967, as we have seen, Gamal Abdel Nasser drove Egypt into a war against Israel that led to the worst defeat in Egyptian history.

Within a few days, Israel managed to crush the Egyptian army and to seize East Jerusalem, Sinai, Gaza, the West Bank and the Golan Heights. But when Nasser announced that he was stepping down, millions of Egyptians went out onto the street to declare their attachment to the leader, based on the logic that the defeat had been brought about by a great American conspiracy. Nasser reassumed power in order to rebuild the army, and the media trumpeted the new Nasserite slogan, "No Voice Louder than the Sound of Battle",[12] meaning that any talk of democratic reform had to be postponed until the battle was won.

Fourth, a conspiracy theory enables the postponement of democracy. Dictators rarely say that they prefer autocratic rule over democracy. A strongman generally speaks in great detail about the circumstances his country is passing through as if it is the circumstances that prevent the present application of democracy. He then emphasises that as soon as he succeeds in foiling the conspiracy and putting an end to the conspirators, he will step down and open the arena for real democratic competition. However, he says, his duty as a leader does not allow him to do this while conspirators are still lying in wait to act against the homeland. A conspiracy theory is usually used successfully as an argument to delay the institution of any democratic reforms.

Fifth, a conspiracy theory provides justification for repression. As the nation is exposed to a great conspiracy, the strongman finds himself obliged to take extraordinary measures to protect the nation and its citizens. These extraordinary measures, which a dictator generally refers to in his speeches in a fleeting and arcane way, generally mean not only the arrest and torture of thousands of people in order to extract confessions from them but also 'disappearances' and extrajudicial killings. A broad section of the general public will completely overlook these crimes or perhaps justify them out of fear of the great conspiracy being waged against their homeland.

Sixth, a conspiracy theory facilitates dehumanisation. In 1920, Hitler gave another impassioned speech in which he spoke about an unnamed group of people who he claimed were destroying Germany for their own interests. At that moment, a man in the audience stood up and started shouting with great emotion, "He means the Jews! The Jews!"[13] That man, like thousands of Nazis, jumped to his feet to blame the Jews without thinking for a moment that a Jew could be a person like him, with a spouse and children. He simply considered a Jew to be just one individual within the whole group of enemy conspirators. Those who participated actively in the persecution that led to the Holocaust, as well as those who did so passively, did not think of Jews as people like themselves but as a group of hostile evildoers who needed to be exterminated.

While I was writing my novel *Chicago*, I was reading about the Vietnam War and I remember coming across an instruction for soldiers from the US army top brass. It read along the lines of, "When shooting an adversary, do not look into his eyes." There is no clearer example of dehumanisation. If you think that the people you are killing are your enemies, it is much easier to shoot them dead. But if you looked into their eyes, you would see not an enemy but a human. You may see a young man, an ordinary person like yourself, and perhaps then you might imagine his mother's grief if you killed him, or imagine him cuddling his children if he returned home. You would not then be able to open fire on him, because you would realise the enormity of the crime you would be committing. To dehumanise the enemy is the first step in any act of killing or terrorist atrocity. The Islamist extremist who goes into a café in a Western capital with the intention of opening fire on people he does not know would not be able to carry out that operation if he thought of his victims as human beings who each have a life like his own. He kills them because he can dehumanise them as simply 'enemies of Islam'.

The US reserve soldier Lynndie England became notorious for her role in the Abu Ghraib torture and prisoner abuse scandal, when she had a colleague take photographs of naked detainees as she stood next to them grinning for the camera with a cigarette in her mouth. When she finished her prison sentence, she maintained that she had done nothing wrong, insisting, "Saying sorry is admitting I was guilty and I'm not. I was just doing my duty."[14] The same logic was applied by the American navigator Theodore 'Dutch' Van Kirk, who was part of the crew that dropped a nuclear bomb on Hiroshima on 6 August 1945, killing 80,000 people in one fell swoop. In his later years, he stated in newspaper interviews, "Under the same circumstances, yes, I would do it again … We were fighting an enemy."[15]

The conspiracy theory is among the most dangerous symptoms of the dictatorship syndrome inasmuch as it allows the dictator a free hand and enables him, finally, to rid himself of any opposition. It also pushes the general population towards accepting and perhaps supporting the most heinous crimes of repression. At the same time, the spread of a conspiracy theory leads to a confusion of the people's collective mind and prevents them from seeing the truth, no matter how blatantly obvious it might appear to outsiders. People who have lived their whole lives in the shadow of a conspiracy theory find it difficult to own up to their own mistakes and prefer to blame others. They find some comfort in interpreting current events as part of a conspiracy, as it frees them from having to feel any responsibility for failure and dispels their sense of helplessness.

In Egypt, the struggle for power between the Islamists and the military has gone on for decades, with both sides accusing the other of being CIA agents.[16] Egyptian state media outlets, which are run by the intelligence services, have spread the rumour that the 2011 revolution that brought down the dictator Hosni Mubarak was in fact no more than a great Masonic plot to destroy Egypt and divide the country into statelets.[17] This was supposedly proven by the fact that some of the young revolutionaries wore armbands that, in the eyes of the state media, are an incontrovertible Masonic symbol. Moreover, some of the revolutionary movements put the image of a clenched fist on their banners – again, according to the Egyptian media, an undeniable Masonic symbol.[18]

What is surprising is just how many of the Egyptian intelligentsia fall for this drivel. For all the bloodshed and disappointed hopes, the uprisings of the Arab Spring that began in late 2010 represent a real attempt to rid the region of dictatorship and of the retrograde ways of thinking that various dictatorships have implanted in Arab society. A revolution, at its core, is no more than an attempt to find a cure for the dictatorship syndrome.

5

The spread of the fascist mindset

Tata Zaki, an Egyptian fashion model, was considered one of the most beautiful women in Egypt in the 1950s. She married a much older, wealthy and famous lawyer before falling madly in love with a handsome young aristocrat who had connections to the now ex-royal family. When she told her husband she wanted a divorce so that she could marry her new boyfriend, he refused point blank, so she moved out. Up to this point the story is quite ordinary and could happen anywhere and at any time. However, Zaki took her problem to the renowned journalist Mustafa Amin, owner of the newspaper *Akhbar el-Yom*, who decided that his newspaper's circulation could only benefit from a number of articles under the headline, "Flight of the Most Beautiful Woman in Egypt".[1]

This was in 1960, and Egypt was firmly under the rule of Gamal Abdel Nasser, who had abolished the democratic system and rival parties and had all his opponents thrown into prison.[2] Nasser was angered by the public interest in Zaki's predicament, just as he was greatly irritated by some of the caricatures drawn by the cartoonist Hijazi in the magazine *Sabah al-Kheir* lampooning a cuckolded husband who discovers his wife's lover hiding in the wardrobe.

Nasser reacted by placing all Egyptian newspapers under state ownership, appointing the former owners to senior positions. In a meeting with the editors-in-chief some years after the nationalisation order, Nasser stated:

> In this act of nationalisation, it is not our aim to take control of the edifices of the press. We have to build a socialist society that is free of exploitation, but the society we wish to build is not one of rich people's clubs and nightlife. That is not Egypt under any circumstances. [The real] Egypt is the Egypt of the villages – which have real problems and about which we should be writing. Anyone who wants to write about our country should go to the villages and see the real agony of Egyptians. The press must be in the service of the people of our country, in the service of the authentic and organic society to which we belong. The press must help to create a social- ist society. We cannot build up the public sector and have some journalist writing against the public sector. There have been announcements in the press which do not accord with the dignity of our country and reports supplied by foreign embassies have become a fixed item in our newspapers. As journalists, you are conscripts in the service of the country. Let any journalist who does not believe in a cooperative, socialist society, say 'I am not a believer' and he can stay at home.[3]

The odd thing about this is that the newspaper owners were the first to give their fervent support to the nation- alisation decree. But were they really being sincere? It is difficult to imagine that a journalist, or an entrepreneur who had struggled for years to become a newspaper owner, would feel any sense of joy as the state expropriated their newspaper – so why would they have supported the decree? Quite simply, it was because they had not forgotten what had happened a few years earlier to their colleague Ihsan Abdel Quddous, editor-in-chief and owner of the magazine *Rose al-Yusuf*.

Quddous was an outstanding political journalist as well as a close friend of Nasser's. In 1954, after the army took power, Quddous wrote an article in *Rose al-Yusuf* entitled "The Secret Society that Governs Egypt".[4] He demanded that members of the secret military organisation the Free Officers, who had carried out the 1952 *coup d'état*, should resign from the army and form political parties prior to elections. He also called for the return of democracy. Quddous was immediately arrested at his home by the military police and spent 100 days in a military prison, during which time he was subjected to torture and various other forms of brutal treatment. The day he was released, he was surprised by a telephone call from Nasser, who chuckled as he asked, "Have you learned some manners yet or do you need a little more time?"[5]

Nasser then invited Quddous to dinner at his house and apologised for having had him arrested, stating that the country could not allow journalists to rock the boat. This episode shows to what extent Nasser was prepared to bring down anyone who wrote something he did not like, even a close friend like Quddous. This must have been in the minds of the newspaper owners when they gave their enthusiastic support to Nasser's nationalisation of the press.

A similar situation occurred 54 years later when Abdel

Fattah el-Sisi concentrated power in his own hands and the intelligence services gained complete control over the media.[6] El-Sisi stated unequivocally, "The role of the national media is to highlight the state's achievements, to spread hope and maintain the morale of the citizens. If the media behave otherwise, they are no more than a tool for the destruction of the state, and that we will never allow."[7]

A dictator does not recognise the media as a means of conveying the truth or expressing various points of view, but rather as a weapon for getting the masses to support the leader. What the leader by his very nature stipulates is that the people must all rally behind one vision and one opinion. This idea of a 'unilateral vision for all' is the *leitmotif* of all dictatorships.

On 10 May 1933, in the Opernplatz in Berlin, the Nazi Student Union burnt up to 25,000 books by scores of authors including Fyodor Dostoyevsky, Ernest Hemingway, Victor Hugo, Leo Tolstoy and André Gide. As the book burning continued, the Nazi minister of propaganda, Joseph Goebbels (1897–1945), addressed the thousands of students:

> The era of an exaggerated Jewish intellectualism is now at an end and the German revolution has cleared a path for the German character ... This revolution did not come from above; it erupted from below. It is therefore in the best sense of the word the execution of the will of the people. Here the worker stands next to the bourgeoisie, student next to the soldier and apprentice; here the intellectual stands next to the proletarian.[8]

In the Soviet Union, we find the same iron censorship, with literature, cinema and the media being directed to publish only socialist thought and create the 'new Soviet man'.[9] Reactionary books whose content went against the Soviet scheme therefore had to be taken out of circulation. In 1923, Nadezhda Krupskaya, the wife of Vladimir Lenin, put together a list of books that she thought the Soviet masses should not read, including the Qur'an, the Old Testament and the works of Immanuel Kant, René Descartes and Tolstoy. When asked the reason for banning Kant, she replied peremptorily, "The masses do not read Kant."[10]

During the era of Joseph Stalin, who ruled the Soviet Union for three decades (1922–1953), newspaper censorship became harsher and a ban was placed on any book considered to contain reactionary thinking. Films with 'positive content' were also produced with the aim of engendering the new Soviet man, a good example being a film that Stalin himself liked. It was called *The Party Card*, produced by Ivan Pyriev and completed in 1936 during a campaign for people to renew their party membership cards. Losing a party membership card was a sign of disrespect and a serious and sanctionable crime. In the film, the young Anka realises that she has lost her party membership card and then discovers that her husband is a former landowner and anti-revolutionary who has stolen her card for use in an operation to assassinate an important communist. In the last scene, Anka's husband asks her to forgive him, but she hands him over to the authorities so that he can be punished appropriately for his dreadful act.

The situation was somewhat similar in fascist Italy,

the difference being that the dictator, Benito Mussolini (1883–1945), started out in life as a journalist and, when in opposition as a politician, was harshly critical of censorship[11] until he took power and censored any ideas deemed politically incorrect by the fascists. Likewise Saddam Hussein, the Iraqi dictator, controlled all the media in order to forge the political consciousness of the Ba'ath Party members who believed in Arab nationalism. However, he also looked beyond the media and held conferences in 2000 and 2003 to discuss with the Iraqi literati how their stories and novels should underpin Arab nationalist ideals.

In religious dictatorships the situation is no better, and censorship in countries such as Iran, Sudan and Saudi Arabia is harsh, encompassing cinema, television, the press and book publishing (both fiction and non-fiction). As well as imposing political censorship, religious rule generally also extends government control to include a form of moral censorship in order to ensure that cultural output does not offend against religious rulings or public virtue.

These examples show us that a dictator always aims to have complete control over the consciousness of the masses and the way they think. He generally brings this about as follows.

First, he eliminates any independent sources of information. He does this by taking complete control of the media, jamming foreign radio broadcasts, closing down any news sites that do not submit to control by the security apparatus and by controlling, blocking or shutting down the various forms of social media.

Second, he mobilises the people against enemies and conspirators. As detailed in the previous chapter, a dictator always adopts a conspiracy theory, and he uses the media to mobilise the full support of the masses in defence of the nation (or the religion) by depicting his opponents as a group of traitors and agents of hostile intelligence agencies being paid to destroy the state. The aim here is character assassination, so that the people will neither trust the voices of the opposition nor listen to their opinions.

Once a dictator has gained full control of the media, he can go on to create an 'alternative truth'. At this point, the line between what is actually happening and the media's false version of events becomes blurred. In this way, a dictator can convince the masses of his heroic achievements – imaginary as they may be – and prevent them from hearing about his administrative failures, the results of his specious policies or the suffering meted out to the thousands of victims of his oppressive practices.

This leads us to ask the following question: if a dictator has complete control of the state apparatus – including the army, the police, the judiciary, the state prosecution service and the civil and military intelligence agencies – why should he be so insistent upon closing down all means of expression? As he has total control over the state, what harm could it do him to leave some space, however small, for those whose opinions differ from his?

The answer is that a dictator always considers himself the owner of the absolute truth and, in his self-inflated vision of himself, he cannot actually understand how it could be that anyone would not go into raptures over his ingenuity and genius or would feel the need to hold a different opinion or criticise his policies. The only explanation that accords with the narcissism of a dictator is that his opponents are the agents of foreign intelligence agencies trying to undermine the country and bring down the state. As a dictator considers himself the only representative of the nation and the people, he sets about oppressing and abusing his opponents without the slightest feeling of guilt using the panoply of methods available to him. These include arrest, torture and killing – practices that, unacceptable as they may be to morality and the law, he deems of vital national interest and that have been made necessary due to the 'dangers' stemming from the conspiracies aimed at the nation. In addition, a dictator may wish to change his mind – as Hosni Mubarak eventually did in 2006 in proposing to change the constitution. Any alternative line of thought should therefore also be exclusively his own.

A dictator sees his people in two contradictory ways. There is the theoretical meaning that rings out in a dictator's speeches in which he gives a central place to the people, always singing the praises of their genius and their astonishing ability to understand and read a given situation so correctly that they can distinguish between nationalists and traitors. However, on the practical level, a dictator has absolutely no faith in the ability of the people to think independently, and he considers that an article or television programme that presents opposing thoughts has the potential to stir up the masses against his regime. This underestimation of the people is perfectly consistent with the concept of a paternalistic dictator. You love your children, but you would never trust their ability to manage things alone. Consequently, you try to keep harmful thoughts from their minds and to prevent them from falling into bad company. Accordingly, a dictator views the people somewhat differently to the way he praises them in his speeches. A dictator believes that his complete control of the press, culture and education – of anything that can form or inform the public consciousness – is the *sine qua non* of his continuation in power.

In the end, a dictator will bring about what he wants. Thanks to the brainwashing of the masses, new generations will arise who will see everything as the dictator wishes – generations who know nothing other than political subjection to the will of the strongman, who are unthinking and unable to express a divergent opinion. With an absence of any political will and a complete psychological reliance on the strongman, those who have grown up in authoritarian societies will be afflicted with another symptom of the dictatorship syndrome, that of 'the fascist mindset', whereby the germ of fascism spreads out from the governing system and the media to the 'good citizen'. In turn, the good citizen becomes a mini-dictator who manifests fascist attitudes in their daily life. A good citizen who has grown up under an authoritarian regime has not been accustomed to listening to opposing views and cannot perceive the various sides of an argument, nor can they form any opinion that diverges from the one truth they are fed by the media or at work, in the mosque or at school. They believe that for every issue there is only one truth, and they cling on to this truth, defending it stringently.

In medicine, when we study a disease, we compare samples from healthy tissue with those from diseased tissue so that we can observe its nature. Egyptian society would serve well for a study of fascism as a symptom of dictatorship. During the first half of the twentieth century, despite the British occupation (which ran from 1882 until 1956) and the ongoing attempts by the king to monopolise power, Egypt witnessed an unprecedented state of intellectual tolerance: when the first Egyptian constitution was being drafted in 1923, the text of an article stating that "freedom of religion is guaranteed to all Egyptians" was amended to read "freedom of belief is guaranteed to all Egyptians",[12] because the drafters of the constitution felt that the word 'religion' was usually restricted to those who believed in organised religion, whereas the word 'belief' encompassed both believers and non-believers. Their logic in making this amendment was that the Egyptian state needed to defend the rights of its citizens even if they were atheists.[13]

In 1926, Taha Hussein, a professor at Cairo University, published a book entitled *On Pre-Islamic Poetry* in which he applied Cartesian doubt, or methodological scepticism, to Islamic history and came to the conclusion that many of the poems considered to belong to the pre-Islamic period were actually more recent forgeries and had erroneous attributions. He wrote that these poems were written after the advent of Islam by unknown authors who claimed that the verses were 'pre-Islamic'. The book angered the clerics and some other religious people who thought that Hussein had shown disrespect to and insulted the religion of Islam itself, and a complaint of 'insulting Islam' was filed against him. However the public prosecutor, Muhammad Nour, held an intense discussion with the accused. In his opinion, Hussein had published his academic research with no intention of insulting the religion and therefore there was no case against him, so he was released without charge.

This sort of religious and intellectual tolerance was a mark of that age, and many more examples can be found. In 1937, for instance, the mathematician and writer Ismail Adham wrote a book called *Why am I an Atheist?* in which he described his journey towards atheism and stated that he was as firm a believer in atheism as any other believer in religion. Adham was neither put on trial nor subject to any oppressive measures, and his books were not withdrawn from the market. The only reactions came from an Islamic scholar called Ahmed Zaki Abu Shadi, who wrote a rebuttal in a pamphlet entitled "Why I am a Believer",[14] and Muhammad Farid Wajdi, who also wrote a long article in response with the title "Why is he an Atheist?"[15] – both also published in 1937. Egyptians followed this public intellectual debate about atheism and faith without a single citizen demanding that books by atheists be banned or the authors put on trial.

Another incident is recounted by Dr Rashad Rushdi, professor of English literature at Cairo University, which took place when he was a student in the 1940s. At that time, the professor of literary criticism was known for his Marxist leanings; in his lectures, he referred to socialist realism as a literary doctrine and emphasised the need for literature to highlight the truth about the class struggle and the fact that the will of the masses would triumph in the end. The young Rushdi was not a fan of socialist realism, as he considered that its overly rigid ideological frame killed off any spontaneity or aesthetic features in literature. During his oral examination at the end of the year, the Marxist professor asked him, "What do you think about socialist realism?"

Rushdi reflected for a moment and asked the professor, "Do you want me to speak about socialist realism the way you did in your lectures?"

The professor replied, "I want to hear your opinion, not mine."

Rushdi poured out his searing criticism of socialist realism, pulling no punches when it came to listing its faults and the danger it posed to aesthetic values in literature. The examination came to an end and Rushdi was certain that he had failed because he had verbally demolished the professor's favourite literary school. However, when the results came out, he was surprised to find that he had come first in the oral examination. When Rushdi went to thank him, the professor smiled and said, "I'm here to teach you how to think and defend your opinions. Your defence of your critique of socialist realism was excellent – even if I didn't agree with a single word of it."

When reading about these incidents, we Egyptians who have grown up in a country contaminated by military dictators can hardly believe that our grandfathers could have enjoyed such a healthy degree of tolerance. But Egypt lost this after the military took power in 1952 and has since set a whole arsenal of laws that impede freedom of expression,[16] criminalise atheism and "violating public decency",[17] with writers and thinkers in prison for having shown "contempt of religion".[18] This criminalisation of thought is determined by the military authorities with the tacit acceptance and support of most Egyptians.

In April 2000, the newspaper *al-Sha'ab* – the paper of the Egyptian Islamic Labour Party and, from 1987 when the party adopted an Islamist position, the mouthpiece of the Islamists – published a sensationalist leading article under the headline, "Will you remain faithful unto death?" The headline referred to a historical tradition practised by soldiers in the armies of Islam before the start of a battle, when they would make an oath to their leader to fight "until victory or death". The reason the newspaper was asking readers to pledge their loyalty in this way was that a novel had been published that the newspaper thought contained a slight against Islam. The book, by the Syrian novelist Haidar Haidar, was called *A Banquet of Seaweed*, and it had first been published in Damascus in 1982 without arousing much interest. But when it was republished 18 years later by the Egyptian Ministry of Culture, *al-Sha'ab* objected strongly to some of the expressions used by one of the novel's protagonists, an Iraqi member of the Communist Party who flees to Algeria where he has an affair with an Algerian woman.

As the Iraqi is an atheist, it is only natural that he uses some anti-religious phraseology. However, this 'blasphemy' raised an enormous hue and cry, and people raged against both the novel and the Ministry of Culture for publishing a book that slighted Islam. *A Banquet of Seaweed* became Egypt's main preoccupation: Muslim Brotherhood members of parliament expressed their anger at it and Islamists from Al-Azhar University organised huge demonstrations in other Egyptian universities.[19] Preachers in mosques throughout the country demanded that the Egyptian masses make their religion victorious over the atheist protagonist of the novel, with ever louder voices calling for the novel to be withdrawn and for those responsible for its publication to be put on trial. The Islamic

Research Group of Al-Azhar University even issued a statement regarding the novel in which it declared, "This novel incites infringement of the Sharia [Islamic law] and represents a grotesque departure from public morals because it encourages sex outside marriage and is itself a slight against God and his Prophet."[20] The statement went on to condemn the Ministry of Culture for publishing the novel. The book was subsequently withdrawn from the market and the official responsible for publishing it was fired and indeed sent for trial.

The odd thing amid all the fuss is that none of these people who were so angered by the novel actually understood, or perhaps they refused to understand, that a novelist is not responsible for the views of his protagonists. One of the very first principles of literary theory is that each protagonist acts according to their own logic, and an atheist character will thus express anti-religious feelings just as a believing character will speak positively about faith. In any case, it is not up to readers to hold a novelist accountable for the opinions of their fictional characters. But perhaps the oddest thing of all is that most of those who savaged the novel had not even read it. Hosts of talk show programmes had a never-ending succession of strange exchanges with the public. Aping the voice of the dictator, angry viewers called in demanding that the novel be pulled from the market immediately, but when asked by the host whether the caller had read the book, the member of the public would generally answer that they would never be able to bring themselves to read anything that slighted their religion. This episode, in medical language, demonstrates an acute exacerbation of a chronic disease.

After decades of military dictatorship, this fascist mindset has spread among Egyptians like a plague. If you look through the letters pages in the Egyptian newspapers, you will always find a reader ranting on about some film or novel because it is 'anti-religion' or offends certain sensibilities. The writer does not just express their anger, but always concludes with the demand that the film should not be screened or that the book should be withdrawn. They cannot grasp that what does not appeal to them may well appeal to others because the culture in which they have grown up only accepts one version of the truth when it comes to politics, and that applies to literature, art and higher education to list just a few examples.

When I was accepted to the Faculty of Dentistry of Cairo University in 1976, I had to spend a year in the School of Science in order to acquire the basic scientific knowledge needed for dentistry. There, the professor of natural chemistry was a bearded Muslim and his forehead bore a prayer mark, or *zebiba* – another outward sign of his piety. In our first lecture, he discussed the material he was going to teach. The moment he walked into the hall for our second lecture, he snatched up the microphone and called out one student's name. When told he was absent, the professor stated, "I knew that boy was a communist. When you see him, tell him he has failed in natural chemistry. I'll fail him and any of you I discover to be a communist."

We were all intimidated into total silence. We were young students who had just finished school, and we learnt a number of lessons from this incident. First, that the professor was in communication with the security service – how else could he have known the political leanings of one of our fellow students? Second, that his outward signs of piety – his beard and the *zebiba* – would not prevent him from committing an act of injustice against any student he should choose. Third, that staying back a year or passing our examinations did not depend solely on how much we worked and studied but also on toeing the correct political line.

I then spent five years being indoctrinated into believing that there were no 'points of view' to be had about the 'one truth' communicated to us by our professors. We all had to try to memorise what the professor said so that we could repeat it verbatim in our exams. The professor of organic chemistry, for example, would laugh out loud as he told us that if a man swallowed a mouse he would not be able to digest it because its skin is covered in indigestible amino acids. Then, in the oral exam, he liked to surprise the students by asking, "What would happen if you swallowed a mouse?" If the student could repeat the professor's words from the lecture, they would be given high marks. If they were shocked or confused, they would be marked down for not having attended the lectures. That is how we learnt that it was more important to attend the professor's lectures and to memorise his witty remarks than to acquire scientific knowledge.

Having reluctantly learned this trick, I graduated with honours and found a job as a resident in the oral surgery department. There you could very clearly see the influence of military rule as an army-like hierarchy was present everywhere, including in the department itself. Authority in the surgery department was not synonymous with responsibility as much as with the ability to abuse subordinates. Every person in the hierarchy took abuse from the one above them and then took it out on the person below. The abuse started from the head of department and was passed down through the professor, assistant professor, teacher, assistant teacher, instructor, resident and junior dentist. Those in this last category were the youngest and lowest in status, and they had to put up with being bullied by everyone. I remember having a discussion with one of the assistant teachers in the department (two rungs above me). I was certain of my opinion on some scientific subject, but he was so insistent on his that I suggested asking one of the more senior professors in the department. We asked one to adjudicate the matter, and I gave him a précis of the argument and the two differing opinions without saying whose was whose.

The professor smiled and asked the assistant teacher which was his opinion. He then fixed me with a cold stare and warned me, "As far as you're concerned, whatever he says is right. He's an assistant teacher and you're just a resident. In this department, whoever is senior is right."

The spread of the fascist mindset is one of the entrenched symptoms of the dictatorship syndrome.

6

The dislocation of the intellectual

"Whenever I hear the word 'culture', I reach for my pistol." This sentence, falsely attributed to the Nazi minister of propaganda, Joseph Goebbels, arguably epitomises a dictator's approach to culture.[1] A dictator generally views intellectuals with a mixture of contempt and mistrust. He considers himself the leader of a nation, a creator of history and a man of great deeds, whereas intellectuals, in his opinion, are no more than verbose pedants who live in a hypothetical world and are incapable of carrying out the simplest of tasks. In the dictator's view, intellectuals make unsatisfying and unconvincing claims to knowledge; they speak when they should remain silent and occasionally pose inconvenient questions. They are driven by ostentation and a passion for futile argumentation, criticising and making observations about subjects of which they know nothing.

But for all that, even if the dictator deems them vain and impotent, intellectuals still represent a danger because they can influence public opinion. An intellectual's views, even if dismissed by a dictator as piffle and claptrap, can spread confusion among the masses and lead them to question the dictator's intentions and abilities. A dictator – who, as we have seen, carefully and rigorously shapes his people's general consciousness – will not, under any circumstances, allow his efforts to be undermined by a writer or public intellectual. On the other hand, a writer or public intellectual living in an authoritarian state finds themselves in a predicament if they can see the human values they defend being violated by the dictator. At that point, there are few choices open to them, and they can be summed up as outlined in this chapter.

The intellectual who resists

When Adolf Hitler gained power in 1933, Thomas Mann, one of the most important German authors at the time, was abroad with his wife on holiday. His friends warned him against returning to Germany for his own safety. Mann stayed in exile for three years, during which time he neither wrote nor uttered a word against Nazism. Whether or not Mann feared Hitler, he was terrified of losing the love of his German readers who had been so afflicted by the fever of Nazism that they could no longer take to their hearts anyone who criticised it – even a great writer like Mann.

After three years, the writer's conscience overcame any worries about his popularity and, on 3 February 1936, he published a response to a piece about German authors in exile written by a Nazi critic in the *Neue Zürcher Zeitung*. In his article, Mann made public his opinion of Hitler for the first time:

> The deep conviction … that nothing good for Germany or the world can come out of the present German regime, has made me avoid the country in whose

spiritual tradition I am more deeply rooted than are those who for three years have been trying to find the courage to declare before the world that I am not a German, and I feel to the very depths of my heart that I have done the right thing in the eyes of my contemporaries and of posterity.[2]

Mann paid an enormous price for taking such a stance. The Nazis declared war on him: his assets in Germany were confiscated, Bonn University withdrew the honorary degree they had conferred upon him 17 years earlier and, finally, he was stripped of his German citizenship.

Worse, however, happened to the German writer Erich Maria Remarque. Remarque's works were among the many publicly burned and banned by Goebbels in 1933 and, though the author left Germany for Switzerland, his youngest sister, Elfriede Scholz, stayed behind with her husband and two children. In 1943, the Nazi government arrested her. After a trial in the *Volksgerichtshof* (Hitler's extra-constitutional 'People's Court'), Scholz was found guilty of "undermining morale" for stating that she considered the war lost. Court President Roland Freisler declared, "Your brother is unfortunately beyond our reach ... you, however, will not escape us."[3] Scholz was beheaded on 16 December 1943, and her family was reportedly billed for the cost of her prosecution, imprisonment and execution.

Another prominent example is Russian writer Aleksandr Solzhenitsyn. When the authorities in the Soviet Union discovered that Solzhenitsyn had expressed a negative opinion about Joseph Stalin in a private letter to a friend, he was arrested forthwith, tried and sentenced to eight years in prison in 1945.[4] After his release, Solzhenitsyn became an open critic of the government.[5] Similarly, in August 1936 during the civil war in Spain, the forces of Francisco Franco (1892–1975) arrested Federico García Lorca at a friend's house in Granada. Three charges were laid against him: being "a Socialist, and a freemason" and for "engaging in homosexual and abnormal practices".[6] The soldiers found it unnecessary to hold a trial: they shot and buried him without further ado.

Likewise, the Italian philosopher Antonio Gramsci was an opponent of Benito Mussolini's regime, and he paid the price for his stance: Gramsci was arrested on 9 November 1926 by the police. His prosecutor in the resulting trial declared, "We must stop this brain working for twenty years."[7] Gramsci was initially sentenced to five years' imprisonment, and this was extended by a further 20 the following year.

Gramsci's health deteriorated in prison. "His teeth fell out, his digestive system collapsed so that he could not eat solid food ... he had convulsions when he vomited blood, and suffered headaches so violent that he beat his head against the walls of his cell."[8] An international campaign was mounted for his release and, despite being moved from prison to a clinic in 1933, Gramsci did not receive sufficient medical care. He died on 27 April 1937, aged 46.

The intellectual who gives his support

The Chilean poet Pablo Neruda was a lifelong admirer of Stalin, and in 1953 he was awarded the International Stalin Prize for Strengthening Peace Among Peoples. Despite mounting criticism of Stalin after his death and the Soviet Communist Party's condemnation of the terror practised by Stalin against both his enemies and his colleagues, Neruda never levelled a single word of criticism against him. The Mexican poet Octavio Paz, who admired Neruda's great talent, nonetheless criticised this stance:

> When I consider … Neruda and other famous Stalinist writers and poets, I feel the gooseflesh that I get from reading certain passages of [Dante's] *Inferno*. No doubt they began in good faith … But insensibly, commitment by commitment, they saw themselves becoming entangled in a mesh of lies, falsehoods, deceits and perjuries, until they lost their souls.[9]

In 1925, the Italian Conference of Fascist Culture issued a statement in favour of the fascist government and in support of the violence practised by the blackshirts against their political adversaries.[10] A group of well-known writers and intellectuals put their names to the statement. The renowned playwright Luigi Pirandello did not attend the conference but had already written a year earlier to declare his full support for fascism, stating, "If Your Excellency considers me worthy, I will deem it the highest honor to be one of the party's humblest and most obedient followers."[11] Unlike Neruda, however, Pirandello's enthusiasm for fascism soon waned and just two years later, in 1927, he tore up his membership card in front of the secretary-general of the Fascist Party and lived the rest of his life under surveillance by the secret police.

When the Cuban revolution was victorious and Fidel

Castro (1926–2016) gained power in 1959, he was supported by some of the greatest names in the world of literature, such as the Peruvian Mario Vargas Llosa, the Mexican Carlos Fuentes, the Colombian Gabriel García Márquez and Julio Cortázar from Argentina. But though these great writers soon lost their enthusiasm for Castro and withdrew their support as a result of the repressive measures he instituted against the people in Cuba, García Márquez remained faithful until the end. He came in for strong criticism due to Castro's dictatorship and the crimes he committed against his opponents. Those who defend García Márquez assert that he made use of his friendship with Castro to persuade him to release a number of political prisoners.[12] However critics of García Márquez do not accept this, and they consider the García Márquez–Castro friendship a black mark against his name, as it is unseemly for a great writer to be a friend of a tyrant no matter the circumstances. García Márquez continued to defend his friendship, claiming that Castro was one of the nicest people he had ever met,[13] that he was a great intellectual and that he was such an insightful reader of literature that he would send Castro the drafts of his novels so that he could incorporate his comments before delivering the book to the publisher.[14]

The intellectual appeaser

Along with those intellectuals who oppose and those who support a dictator, there are some who try to take no position: they neither give him the chance to take action against them by opposing him, nor do they ignore any misgivings and support him.

This category includes the Russian Boris Pasternak, who lived under Soviet rule but was not the subject of any repressive measures. Only towards the end of his life, when he completed his famous novel *Doctor Zhivago* (1957), did he risk his freedom. He had the manuscript smuggled out of the country and to the Italian publisher Giangiacomo Feltrinelli, joking, "You are hereby invited to watch me face the firing squad."[15] The events in the novel take place between 1903 and 1929, years of privation and bloody unrest in Russia, and Pasternak sets down for us the story of the Bolshevik revolution from the viewpoint of Dr Yuri Zhivago, a physician and poet, who is struggling to find meaning in the human soul. Dr Zhivago, born at the end of the nineteenth century, had completed his medical studies during the First World War. Following the changing political scene and the fall of the imperial Russian regime, political unrest prevails over all sections of society. But rather than focusing on political events, the novel centres on the fate of protagonists who are buffeted by political events on which they can effect not the slightest change. In doing so, Pasternak shows how revolutionary stances and policies change before and after gaining power and illustrates the effect authority has on a person.

The book was published first in Italian, before appearing in English in 1958. It was an instant bestseller, helped in part by a CIA effort to use the book's popularity to expose the realities of life under communism, and this acclaim got the Nobel committee's notice. Pasternak was awarded the Nobel Prize for Literature to the exhilaration of the West and the infuriated humiliation of the USSR.

The consequences were swift and merciless: a smear

campaign, impassioned anti-Pasternak speeches and the threat that Pasternak would be refused re-entry to his home country if he should travel to Sweden to accept his award. Though Pasternak had expressed his delight at receiving the honour days before, he had no choice. On 29 October 1958, he sent a telegram to the Nobel Prize committee, "Considering the meaning this award has been given in the society to which I belong, I must reject this undeserved prize which has been presented to me. Please do not receive my voluntary rejection with displeasure. – Pasternak."[16]

Pasternak had declined under intense pressure from Soviet authorities. But despite his turning down the award, Soviet officials turned on Pasternak, and he was threatened at the very least with expulsion. In response, Pasternak wrote to Soviet Premier Nikita Khrushchev (1894–1971), "Leaving the motherland will equal death for me. I am tied to Russia by birth, by life and work." Though he died within two years, his son accepted the Nobel Prize in his name in 1988.[17]

Other examples of this attitude toward a dictator include the Egyptian novelist Naguib Mahfouz. Mahfouz was 41 years old when the military took power in 1952 and was to live for another 50 years without opposing the military dictatorship once. His ongoing appeasement made him the darling of the regime, and he was given a number of top-level jobs, such as director of the minister of guidance's office, director of censorship in the Bureau of Arts, director of the Foundation for the Support of the Cinema and consultant to the Egyptian General Organization for Cinema and Television. The last position he held in the civil service was that of chairman of the Management Committee of the

Cinema Association. In the early 1970s, Mahfouz retired from the civil service and went to work as a journalist for *Al-Ahram*, the most important state-controlled newspaper in Egypt.

It is notable, however, that his appeasement of dictatorship did not work its way into any of his novels, nor are any of his novels devoid of criticism of authoritarianism when embodied or enacted by one of the protagonists. This device enabled Mahfouz to manoeuvre around the authorities and to avoid criticism by claiming that a novelist is not responsible for the views of the characters he creates. Mahfouz expressed as follows, "I can say with a clear conscience that I said everything I wanted to say in my novels and I expressed all my opinions during the period of Nasser's rule, and those which I felt I could not state openly I communicated through allegory."[18]

The crunch came in 1966 when Mahfouz published *Adrift on the Nile*, which tells the story of a group of friends who meet on a houseboat every night. As they smoke hashish, their talk turns to criticism of the military dictatorship which purports to speak on behalf of a people they have repressed and prevented from having any political participation. The novel greatly irritated Nasser's second-in-command, Field Marshal Abdel Hakim Amer (1919–1967), whom we shall encounter later, who stated that Mahfouz had overstepped a line and needed to be taught a lesson.[19] He was about to issue an order to arrest Mahfouz, but Nasser asked Tharwat Okasha, the minister of culture at the time, for his opinion of the novel. Okasha spoke in favour of Mahfouz, saying that any criticism by Mahfouz was intended for the benefit of the regime and the revolution. Nasser quashed any action against Mahfouz, and the matter came to an end. Mahfouz himself commented on this episode:

> During the era of Abdel Nasser, the authorities trusted to the good intentions in my writing and understood that in my criticism I did not intend to stir up or incite the masses but to write for the good of our country. I believe Abdel Nasser was perfectly aware of that and that is why he intervened on my behalf in the crisis around my novel *Adrift on the Nile* rather than leaving the matter in the hands of an angry Abdel Hakim Amer.[20]

The part-time intellectual

Amid the horrendous repression practised by a dictator against anyone who opposes him, intellectuals often live in fear for their lives and freedom or crave the position and privilege offered by a dictator. They declare their support for the dictator and receive payment in kind, an unwritten contract in which the dictator's reputation is burnished and his noble stance recorded in writing at no cost to himself.

Such intellectuals can opt to take on a part-time campaign for which they adopt some social cause and go on about it with great gusto: take for example the Egyptian critic Gaber Asfour, who wrote about freedom of expression while serving an authoritarian regime in a high government post and who originally accepted the Gaddafi Prize (though he later returned it).[21] In authoritarian systems, we often find regime-compliant intellectuals becoming part-time fighters for causes such as changing the educational syllabus in order to foster greater tolerance, putting an end to child labour or domestic violence, increasing welfare payments for divorced women and salary equality for women.[22] These are all naturally not only worthy causes but indispensable in building a developed and humane society, though we will never be able to make real progress with any social cause if the system of government remains authoritarian. How can an end be brought to domestic violence when citizens, men and women, are every day subjected to beating and torture in prisons?[23] And what is the value of a law promulgated to protect divorced women when any young secret police officer can violate the law? What essential use is any amendment to the law when the judiciary has lost its independence and become a tool for the dictator to do whatever he wishes? How can we put an end to the phenomenon of child labour before we eradicate the poverty that forces children into work in order to provide for their destitute families? How can we put an end to poverty without eradicating the corruption that always issues from a dictatorship? Part-time campaigns will remain a waste of effort; they merely allow an intellectual to salve their conscience by playing some role that makes them look better. True social and cultural change remain dependent on democratic change.

Part-time campaigning, in medical language, is like attempting to treat the symptoms without treating the underlying disease. Such attempts are doomed to fail in medicine as in life. A dictator, on the other hand, generally welcomes part-time campaigning because it creates a false democratic veneer and diverts the efforts of some of society's elite onto issues that do not pose a threat to the dictator's power. It should be noted, too, that democratic societies require work to alleviate social issues, such as child poverty, so such token efforts within a dictatorship can hardly prove effective.

The jobbing intellectual

This collection of stories takes us to remarkable worlds of fertile literary performance and attempts to establish a dazzling panorama of contemporary human hopes and pains. Not only does the author transition from the past to the present, and from the village to the city, but he also takes us in the opposite direction – from the present to the past. I was delighted to read this collection and I would hope that its author finds the time and peace of mind to present us with more new stories to rouse us from the deep slumber in which we find ourselves.

Fouad Qandil (Egyptian writer)

This critical opinion does not review the short story oeuvre of Anton Chekhov or Guy de Maupassant; instead, it refers to a collection of short stories, *Escape to Hell and Other Stories* (1993), written by Muammar Gaddafi. Yes, the same Gaddafi who came to power in Libya in a military coup in 1969 and who kept the country in an iron grip for more than four decades, along the way committing ghastly crimes and causing the death of tens of thousands of innocent Libyans.[24] This disturbed and bloodthirsty dictator suddenly morphed into a literary figure and published various works under the titles "The City", "The Village", "The Earth" and "The Suicide of the Astronaut".

In the opinion of honest literary critics, the anthology did not constitute a literary work by any stretch of the imagination but was instead a collection of hallucinations and the vaguest and most worthless shreds of ideas. They indicate that the author was in need of psychological treatment more than anything else. However, with the aid of huge handouts afforded by Libya's oil revenues, Gaddafi managed to receive critical praise from some of the greatest names in Arabic literature, such as Mohamed Salmawy, president of the Arab Writers' Union, who convened a literary conference in the Libyan city of Sirte in October 2009. At the conference, Salmawy eulogised Gaddafi's immense literary talent, stating that each thought crafted by the genius of Gaddafi merited a conference of its own. Salmawy then presented Gaddafi with the organisation's highest award – the Shield of the Arab Writers' Union.[25]

Gaddafi, incidentally, was well aware that intellectuals could be bought over, enabling him to get whatever he wanted. In 1988, for instance, he established the Al-Gaddafi International Prize for Human Rights, which rewarded entrants for their respect for human rights. The whole affair looked like a farce, particularly as Gaddafi went on to order the execution of 1,500 prisoners in one day on 24 June 1996 in what came to be known as the Abu Salim prison massacre – just one of the many massacres he ordered.

However, Gaddafi kept on setting up awards and later established the Gaddafi Award for Literature with a prize value of $250,000. In 2009, the jury awarded the prize to the Spanish writer Juan Goytisolo, but he nobly refused to accept the prize, stating that his conscience would not allow him to accept funds from the oppressed Libyan people in the form of a prize awarded by a tyrant who had taken power in a military coup.[26] The jury found itself in something of a dilemma and reportedly offered the award to the Nigerian author Chinua Achebe, who turned it down for the same reasons. Finally, the jury found a solution in Asfour, who initially accepted the prize with open arms. At the award ceremony, Asfour gave a speech in which he praised Gaddafi as a ruler, revolutionary and literary personality. He concluded emotionally, "Today I have won one prize three times. Once on behalf of Egypt. Once on behalf of all Arab writers, and once for the nationalism I represent and will cling onto."[27]

Such pathetic hypocrisy has been practised by many intellectuals in Arab countries ruled by authoritarian systems, both royal and military. In Iraq, some poets used to depict Saddam Hussein as the next best thing to God. The Iraqi poet Nassif al-Nasseri wrote:

> Saddam, you are the one we have waited for,
> You our hope,
> You our redeemer,
> You have redeemed our souls and our lives,
> You, our great tent,
> You, our only tent,
> Your sun glints on the Two Rivers,*
> And their suns are ashes.[28]

Another instance of artistic pandering came in 1975, when Saddam Hussein complained of pain in his spine and

---

* Iraq was the 'Land of the Two Rivers' in the national anthem of the time.

his doctors encouraged him to spend some time in hospital. He had a number of Iraqi intellectuals, writers and artists brought to his bedside so that he could recount his political memoirs and his struggle to achieve power. Those gathered around Saddam Hussein's bed pretended to be dazzled by the stories of his struggle. One of them, Abdel Ameer Ma'allah, noted down every word and published his notes in instalments in Iraqi newspapers. He then re-used the material in a 1978 novel about Saddam Hussein's 'heroic acts' entitled *The Long Days*. The book was printed by the million along with many foreign-language editions. It was then decided to turn the novel into a film with an unlimited budget, meaning that the film would be completed no matter what the cost to the public purse.

This open-ended budget seems to have appealed to the Egyptian leftist film director Tewfik Saleh as he agreed to direct the film. But then came the extremely difficult step of casting someone who both looked like the Iraqi dictator and was worthy of taking on his 'great' character. The conditions for playing the role reportedly were that the actor should be proficient in the art of acting, that there was nothing in his past that might sully his reputation, and that he should not have already been filmed playing 'inappropriate' roles that would preclude him from being considered to play the leader. Saleh looked around for a long time until he finally found his ideal in the person of the president's cousin, who looked exactly like the young Saddam Hussein. The director started giving him acting lessons and put a great deal of effort into directing the film. When Saleh sent a copy of the final cut to Saddam Hussein, the leader thanked him and, in addition to lavish payment for the job, offered Saleh and his family unlimited use of one of his presidential villas.

The director then went off to holiday with his family at the villa. The next day, the director of the Cinema Association came to tell him that the leader wanted to see him immediately but would give no further reason. Saleh was terror-struck. He was asked to wait in an ante-room where he noticed an elderly man also waiting, and after a short while they were both told that the leader would see them now. Saleh saw Saddam Hussein, his wife and his ministers watching the film, so he sat down with them until it came to a scene portraying the young leader having been shot in the leg and a doctor having to extract the bullet without any anaesthetic. The young man playing the role of Saddam Hussein winced slightly as the doctor extracted the bullet. At this exact point, Saddam Hussein ordered the screening to be stopped and he turned to Saleh, "This man sitting near you is the doctor who took the bullet out of my leg."

Then he directed a question at the elderly man, "Do you recall seeing me in any pain or displaying the slightest reaction as you removed the bullet from my leg without anaesthetic?"

The doctor of course answered straight away, "No, Sir. Not the least reaction from you."

Saddam Hussein then addressed the film director, "Before you release this film, delete that scene. In real life, Saddam Hussein's face never registers any pain and that's how it should appear in the film."

At this juncture, the minister of information made an effort to calm the atmosphere, "I thought it was a great shot of you, Sir."

"Shut your face," barked Saddam Hussein. "You know nothing!"

What he had demanded was rather difficult technically, but the director went at it doggedly until he managed to delete the offending seconds and splice footage in which the young actor was smiling. This was then followed by the Cinema Association staff being sent around post-haste to make sure that only the amended version would be shown. As a result, millions of Iraqis saw their leader smiling away as the bullet was being extracted.

These snippets of history are obviously absurd, but they lead us to pose some questions: how and why do talented intellectuals become so involved in this type of ingratiation with a dictator? How did culture – which is in its very essence a defence of the truth, justice and freedom – become no more than a craft hired out to anyone who can pay the price? The Egyptian author Salah Eissa in his book *Intellectuals and the Military* (1986) provides an analysis of the personality of the 'jobbing intellectual':

From our youth to our maturity, we have come across types of intellectuals who understand culture to be a sharp tongue, a fluent pen, and who have talent for presenting wrong as right or black as white. They cloak the basest of aims with the noblest of slogans. Unfortunately most of these people are of humble social origins and have clawed a hard and bloody path up the social ladder so that they can be as close as they can to the summit. Once they reach it, they become captivated by the limelight and lose their moral equilibrium. They realise the precariousness of their position, steel themselves and hold on tight. Their teeth chatter as they see the prospect of falling from favour, being ostracised or sent to jail, so they fall in and set about justifying everything their masters do, convincing themselves that culture is a job just like welding, plumbing or carpentry. Just as a tradesman should not refuse to do a job in protest at his foreman, an intellectual should not withhold his trade from any system of government. And in this manner some of them have become courtiers to the sultan, vigorously defending him against those who do not believe in him and changing their positions at the sultan's whim.

These jobbing intellectuals live in a permanent state of anxiety and moral turpitude, being torn between their loyalty to the object of their worship, that is to themselves, and their pathetic sense of shame as they are unable and too cowardly to offer up any defence of what they believe in their hearts to be right and just. They put on a great show of self-righteousness as they sell themselves to the highest bidder, and display pride at the status they allot themselves, which they have crafted at the expense of their every last core value. They resent decent people because they show them up to the public and to themselves and because they symbolise that part of their conscience which they have tried to kill but which refuses to die.[29]

Whatever stance an intellectual takes towards a dictator – whether they oppose him and are exiled, jailed or killed, or whether they appease him and are forced into silence or go against their own conscience and churn out anything for money – whatever the circumstances, when a dictator attains power, intellectuals are displaced from their natural duty to enlighten minds and provide an impetus for intellectual activity. In an authoritarian society there is no room for a serious, independent intellectual because intellectual activity only bears fruit in a free society. The conflicted position of intellectuals under dictatorships is one of the prevalent symptoms of the syndrome.

7

Dictatorship and the predisposing
factors for terrorism

The sparrow seemed deeply unhappy, so God asked, "Why are you so miserable?"

"I'm miserable," the sparrow replied, "because I have put a huge effort into building a nest in that tree, but You, O Lord, have destroyed my nest so I'm now homeless with nowhere to shelter and I'll have to expend all that effort again to build a new nest."

"Don't be downhearted," God answered. "You only saw it as a nest to live in whereas I can see everything. There was a large viper there who was just waiting to ambush you and so I destroyed the nest in order to save your life. Although you think I have wronged you, Sparrow, I have saved you."

The sparrow stopped being sad and began to praise God for his kindness and blessings and set about enthusiastically building a new nest.

This parable, well known within Islam, teaches us that we should not be saddened when a calamity befalls us because it may actually be saving us from an even greater catastrophe known only to God. In this regard, the Qur'an states, "But it is possible that ye dislike a thing which is good for you, and that ye love a thing which is bad for you. But God knoweth, and ye know not" (Qur'an 2:216).[1]

Humankind has always felt the need for religion to offer some explanation as to how we came into this world and where we will go after death. Religion also makes a systematic and clear connection between good and evil, reward and punishment. This gives us some assurance that justice, which does not always come into play during our lifetime, will most certainly be realised after death: those who have done evil will end up being burnt in the fires of hell, and those who have done good will enjoy the blessing of eternal paradise. Moreover, faith in a knowing god provides believers with some consolation when they are struck by a calamity because they believe that God is protecting them from greater ills of which they are unaware but about which God knows, just as with the sparrow in the parable. Faith in a religion teaches a believer human values, something that makes them a better person, but has religion always been the impetus for people to do only good?

Here one might recall the horrific image of masked Islamic State fighters shouting *'Allahu akbar'* before they slaughter their unfortunate shackled victims whose only crime is being non-Muslim.[2] Such savage and horrendous crimes committed under the banner of religion have regrettably been carried out time and time again throughout human history. The French polymath Gustave Le Bon detailed what happened to the Muslims and Jews after the Fall of Granada, which ended Moorish rule in Spain in 1492:

Ferdinand had made a treaty with the Arabs guaranteeing them the right to practise their religion and to use their own language; but 1499 saw the beginning of a period of persecution which was to culminate at the end of the century with their expulsion. It started with forced baptisms, then, even though they had become Christians, they were tried by the Inquisition which consigned as many as possible to the flames. As the operation was proceeding slowly due to the difficulty of burning several million individuals, discussions were held regarding the best way of purging the country of any foreign elements. The Grand Inquisitor and Archbishop of Toledo, a man of great piety, suggested putting to the sword all the unconverted, women and children included. The Dominican Jaime Bleda was even more radical. Since one could never know if all the converts had sincerely accepted Christianity, and as it would be no difficulty for God to distinguish between those who deserved hell or not in the afterlife, the holy man suggested that every last Arab should have his throat slit. Although this measure won the enthusiastic support of the Spanish clergy, the government felt that the victims might not submit so easily and, in 1610, it ordered the expulsion of the Arabs. Hence it was arranged that most of them were cut down as they made their way out of the country. The prominent monk, Bleda, of whom I have spoken earlier, stated with great satisfaction that more than three quarters were killed this way. In just one mass emigration during which 140,000 people were making their way to [North] Africa, 100,000 were massacred.[3]

Le Bon goes on to give examples of horrific crimes committed earlier in history by the crusader armies.* He quotes from an eyewitness, Robert the Monk, who describes the crusaders as behaving "like a frenzied lioness whose cubs have been snatched away from her. They were slicing people to pieces ... and, to accelerate their killing operation, they would hang several Muslims at a time by the same rope."[4] Robert the Monk likewise reports on what the crusaders did in Jerusalem, quoting from Canon Raymond d'Agiles of Puy-en-Velay, "Their behaviour in the holy city was most different from that of the noble Caliph Umar towards the Christians a few centuries earlier ... We could see piles of heads, hands and feet in the roads and open spaces of Jerusalem."[5]

Religion, for all its having taught us its great human values, has often pushed humankind into committing the worst and most brutal crimes. After every terrorist attack in a Western country, journalists scramble to interview the terrorist's neighbours or colleagues who generally state that they were a gentle and nice person and that they could never have imagined them committing such a ghastly crime.[6] So, how does such an apparently gentle person turn into a terrorist?

In the natural sciences, a causal relationship is crucial. In chemistry, for example, we know empirically that when you add A to B you will end up producing C. Such inviolable rules, however, do not carry over into human behaviour:

---

* Editor's note: The Crusades were European military expeditions by Christian countries attempting to wrest control of the Christian holy sites from the Muslims in the Holy Land during the eleventh, twelfth and thirteenth centuries.

the same events under the same circumstances do not necessarily lead to the same results. Hence it is not accurate to speak of the 'causes' of terrorism because any number of causes may lead one person to carry out an act of terrorism while someone else who might be exposed to those same causes does not turn into a terrorist. We should therefore draw back a little and find a better expression than 'the causes of terrorism'. Perhaps a more exact phrase would be 'the predisposing factors for terrorism'.

When present, these predisposing factors make a terrorist incident much more likely to happen. They can be outlined as follows.

Emotional faith

Only two types of religious people choose their faith: those who lived at the time of the prophets and decided to believe them, and those who converted to a different religion that they found more meaningful than their 'birth' religion. Apart from these two types of people, we inherit our religion – or our lack of faith – from our parents. We believe in it from when we are little children, we become emotionally attached to it and, over time, religion becomes a basic part of our memories and our consciousness. We never use intelligence in order to come to a religion, though we do so in order to defend it.

Religion is thus a completely inherited and instinctive belief. We build our peace of mind upon faith in a religion and we rarely allow that to be questioned. You can take the cleverest, most intellectually gifted, most open and tolerant person when it comes to mundane matters, but if the conversation turns to any form of scepticism regarding religion, they can suddenly turn into a fanatic, ever-ready to deny glaring truths, to start spouting baseless and unprovable assumptions and to defend legends and fantasy. They may resort to sterile debate and become arrogant or hostile. They are driven by deep religious feeling and by their instinctive fear of doubt penetrating the firm religious belief upon whose foundation they have built their life and their vision of the world. Therefore, there is no point at all in discussing religion with such believers because their emotions do not allow them, spiritually or intellectually, to undertake a logical re-examination of religious doctrine.

This emotional faith engendered by religion is also a phenomenon of dictatorships. Watch a speech given by any dictator in the modern era and you will not find a single logical argument. A dictator never speaks to the intellect but works on the emotions of the masses who submit completely to their feelings, who do not engage their intellects and instead start to empathise with the dictator. They see him as someone who represents their will, who is their hero and saviour and to whom they will give their support in any decision he should make. The millions of people who stood for hours, shouting themselves hoarse, their hands raw from applauding Adolf Hitler or Benito Mussolini, were not stupid or empty-headed. They had submitted to the dictator's magic spell and had been taken over by an emotional state that eradicated their consciousness and will – a form of mass hypnosis.

As we have seen, in 1958, Gamal Abdel Nasser announced the formation of a union between Egypt and Syria and the establishment of a new state called the United Arab Republic in which Syria was to be the northern province and Egypt the southern. The union lasted until 1961, when a group of Syrian officers rebelled and plotted a coup against Nasser, which led to the secession of Syria. The day after the coup plot was uncovered on 28 September,[7] Nasser gave a speech to thousands of Egyptians in Republic Square in Cairo. The acclamations from the people went on so long and with such enthusiasm that he had to delay the start of his speech. Nasser read out details about the coup in Syria, stating that the plotters were no more than a small group of "reactionaries and imperialist agents" and that the Syrian people still supported the union. He went on:

"Yesterday, the moment I was informed of the coup, I issued an order for the Egyptian armed forces to be moved immediately to Syria to put an end to the plot and to protect the union."

At this point the masses went into a frenzy and started chanting, "We're all your soldiers, Nasser!"[8]

Nasser paused a moment and then continued, "That was my decision yesterday. But I thought the matter over and asked whether an Arab should kill his brother Arab? I could never allow that to happen. So I have issued an order to the Egyptian armed forces to return to Cairo and not to attack the plotters."

People cheered just as wildly at the new decision. What we see here is people cheering loudly for a decision and then for the exact opposite within a few minutes. There is no clearer example of the way emotional belief in a dictator takes hold of people. Like religion, dictatorship plays a role in the control mechanisms used on the masses, numbing their intellects and manipulating their emotions in order to produce blind faith and total submission.

Obsessive belief

When it comes to the more than 4,000 religions estimated to be embraced by humankind, the most devout of each religion believe that they alone have found the right path and that followers of other religions are in error. Speaking generally, for example, Jews do not accept that the real Messiah has come, and Christians believe that Muhammad, the messenger of the Muslims, was in essence not a prophet but a tribal leader and warrior. Muslims, on the other hand, believe that Jews and Christians have falsified their holy books and are therefore in error on matters of true belief, which can only be found in Islam. Add to that the terrible conflicts, mostly bloody, between various branches of the same religion – such as the conflicts between the Shi'a and the Sunnis or the Protestants and Catholics – and we find ourselves face to face with the most dangerous part of religion: obsessive belief.

Islam differentiates between sharia (religious law) and jurisprudence. Sharia signifies the laws revealed by God (in the Qur'an), and jurisprudence means extricating law from sharia and applying it in day-to-day matters. Sharia is divine, and jurisprudence represents the human endeavour of the jurists. Most jurists of Islam deem the evidence of a non-believer (non-Muslim) unacceptable in a case against a Muslim because the 'lesser person' (the non-believer) cannot bear witness against the superior person (the Muslim). Further, they consider that Islam prevents the application of the death penalty against a Muslim if they have killed a non-believer as the soul of a Muslim cannot be compared to that of a non-believer.

This obsession with differentiating between the rights accorded to believers and non-believers has much in common with the way a dictator views the world. Surely these discriminatory juridical rulings bring to mind the slogan "Freedom is for the people; no freedom for the enemies of the people!" that used to ring out under Nasser.[9] Or they recall the steps taken by a dictator to abuse his opponents, the "enemies of the people" – from confiscating their assets and revoking their citizenship to arrest, torture or even death. In dictatorial systems, opponents are dealt with just like disbelievers in the eyes of a religion. Dictatorships and religion also have much in common in the way they have a monopoly on the truth, and in how they abolish the rights of those outside the stockade of belief in a religion or a dictator.

The ideology of violence

There is an enormous difference between a Muslim and an Islamist. A Muslim is an ordinary person who has an attachment to their religion. Their human values are inspired by their religion, and they follow its teachings to do good so that they may gain God's pleasure in this world and enter into paradise after death. An Islamist does not just believe in their religion, but they also believe in the theory of political Islam, which posits that Islam is a religion and a state – in other words, in addition to its role as a religion, Islam is also a political model defined for the establishment of a state. This theory calls upon its followers to wage *jihad* in order to establish a 'caliphate', which is an Islamic state that they believe will inevitably rule the world one day.

Here the gap between a Muslim and an Islamist becomes almost contradictory. A Muslim is generally a peaceable person who lives a normal life and interacts with non-Muslims with respect and tolerance. However, an Islamist is an extremist who has no tolerance for non-Muslims and turns to violence at the drop of a hat. A Muslim shows allegiance to a state and may be left- or right-leaning in their politics, but an Islamist does not believe in nation states or in political thought. They believe that an Islamic state is their religion and that the establishment of an Islamic caliphate is the only type of political thinking for which one must fight against the whole world. Muslims are essentially the victims of Islamists. After every terrorist action carried out by Islamist terrorists, millions of Muslims the world over face trouble in the form of increased surveillance, mistreatment and attacks by right-wing extremists.[10] In fact, statistics confirm that Muslim victims of terrorism far outnumber non-Muslim victims.*[11]

Islamists all share the same ideology and differ only in their tactics: whereas jihadi organisations do not recognise

---

* A 2011 report by the US government's National Counterterrorism Center (NCTC), states this fact clearly, "In cases where the religious affiliation of terrorism casualties could be determined, Muslims suffered between 82 and 97 per cent of terrorism-related fatalities over the past five years." Statistics from the Global Terrorism Database (GTD) at the University of Maryland show that Iraq, Afghanistan and Pakistan – all of which have a mostly Muslim population – were disproportionately affected by terrorism between 2004 and 2013, suffering about half of all terrorist attacks and 60 per cent of fatalities due to terrorist attacks.

democratic methods such as elections or an elected assembly and call for their followers to take up arms, the Muslim Brotherhood* – who had a secret apparatus up until the 1970s and whose mission was to carry out terrorist actions and political assassinations – use democratic methods and take part in elections so that they can achieve power and then monopolise it in order to establish a caliphate. Islamists are, theoretically at least, in a state of war with the non-Muslim world as, without the notion of *jihad*, political Islam would lose its meaning and aim.

The senior 'clerics' of political Islam groom their young followers by preaching a falsified version of history. They teach them, for example, that "when they were truly devoted to their religion, Muslims ruled the world, but when they went against the teachings of the religion, God allowed them to be defeated and to become backward."[12] Nothing could be further from the truth. Throughout the centuries, Muslims have only had rulers who carried out the teachings of Islam for 29 years under the Rightly Guided Caliphs (632–661). All other rulers were simply tyrants who perpetrated injustice, plundered and killed. The man who founded the Abbasid state, for example, Abu al-Abbas (who ruled 750–754), was known far and wide as 'the blood-shedder',[13] an epithet he earned due to the great number of people he killed. In one incident, he killed scores of his Umayyad opponents and had their bodies

---

* Hassan al-Banna (1906–1949) formed the Muslim Brotherhood as a youth group in March 1928 when he was a 22-year-old Arabic schoolteacher in the Suez Canal city of Ismailia. His agenda was anti-colonial and strongly rooted in his faith: to end the British occupation and to set up a state based on principles found in the Qur'an.

covered with rugs. Having ordered food to be brought and set down on the rugs, he is quoted as saying, "By God, I have never eaten such delicious food!"[14] One might also mention that the Ka'ba (the holiest site for Muslims) was destroyed and set alight twice during the Umayyad struggle for power – firstly in 683 and again in 692. The Islamic state was essentially an empire founded on colonialism, intrigue and massacre – like any other empire in the post-classical world.

The Ottoman state, which the Islamists deem to have been a caliphate, was yet another empire founded and maintained by massacres, including the mass slaughter of Christians and Muslims alike. In 1517, when the Ottomans took Cairo, they killed more than 10,000 Egyptian Muslim civilians and rounded up thousands of women and children, demanding their families pay a heavy ransom or they would be turned into servants and slaves.[15] The Ottoman soldiers generally committed these crimes in a state of inebriation, a wine-befuddled haze. This brutal struggle for power led the Muslim jurists to demand that the defeated people give their obedience to the ruler in power in order to avoid armed conflicts, which could then lead to an even greater number of innocent victims, thereby establishing the principle that the defeated obey the man who wields power. In their opinion, therefore, Muslim rule was assumed to come about in two ways: either by the people swearing their allegiance or by them being forcefully subdued.

As for people believing that the early Muslims were all devoted to their religion, that is a great historical fallacy, and there was just as much sexual licence in Baghdad under the Abbasid state in the ninth century as there is

nowadays in New York City. There were wine taverns everywhere, and extramarital sex – as well as homosexuality
– was an accepted fact of life in Abbasid society, which also
evinced the utmost tolerance toward atheists and religious
sceptics.[16] Poems about overcoming religious scruples and
songs in praise of wine and expressing homosexual love are
well-known genres of Arab poetry of that era as we can see
in the odes of the great Abbasid poet Abu Nuwas.[17] It is
undeniable that the Islamic empire provided humankind
with spectacular achievements in the arts and sciences, but
other empires, which were similarly founded on blood, also
produced great civilisational innovation. The existence and
flourishing of an Islamic state were not the expression of
Islamic teachings but were produced by the great energy,
the scientific excellence, the serious intellectual activity, the
perseverance and the achievements that characterise all clas-
sical empires. Whereas the religion of Islam teaches people
to be peaceable and civilised, political Islam is a thoroughly
fascist ideology that is almost identical to any fascist dictatorship anywhere.

A fascist regime comes to power by claiming a total monopoly on the truth, a belief in ethnic or religious superiority
and a reliance on violence to subdue opponents. The lesson
that we can learn from modern Arab history is that Islamist
fascism does not find it easy to grow and acquire followers
in a democratic atmosphere. From 1928, when the Muslim
Brotherhood was established, up until the military coup
that overthrew Egyptian democracy in 1952, the Brotherhood failed to gain any noticeable presence in the Egyptian
parliament with every genuine election resulting in an
overwhelming majority for the Wafd, the largest secular

party in the history of Egypt. The Brotherhood gave their support to the 1952 coup,[18] publicly demanding the dissolution of the democratic system, in the hope of sharing power with the military. However, Nasser turned on them and unleashed successive campaigns of repression. Over the next 60 years, Egyptians have been besieged by two types of fascism: that of the military in power and that of the Islamists trying to wrench power from them.

Belief in collective guilt and dehumanisation

There have been instances where young men have walked into cafés, stations or restaurants in a European city and then screamed out, "This is for the martyrs in Iraq",[19] and blown themselves up or opened fire on people.

This form of crime, in addition to its ghastliness and brutality, reveals a pattern of thinking that I consider to be a predisposing factor for terrorism. These particular terrorists do not recognise individual responsibility, nor do they hold a person solely responsible for their own deeds, as stipulated by laws the world over. They consider all Westerners responsible for the crimes committed by some soldiers against Iraqis and for this reason, among others, they believe that it is their duty as militant Islamists to kill Westerners anywhere as an act of revenge. As well as upholding the principle of collective guilt, terrorists dehumanise their victims, not recognising that each and every one of them has an independent existence. In this instance, Islamist terrorists see Westerners as a group hostile to Muslims who must be eradicated.

Here, again, terrorists and dictators share a similar pattern of thinking. When Hitler spoke about the Jews in his speeches, he was doing just what many terrorists are doing now: holding a whole group responsible for the purported actions of a few. He did not see them as individuals but dehumanised them as an anti-German subspecies. Western fascist groups have adopted the same pattern of thinking when their mobs hit the streets in search of a Muslim to beat up because they hold all Muslims responsible for the actions of a terrorist simply by dint of a common religion.[20] Fascists, dictators and terrorists all apply the same logic: that of collective guilt and dehumanisation.

Enmity to the West

"The West is hostile to Islam and is trying to wipe it out."

Variations on this sentence are preached from the pulpit in thousands of mosques that accommodate the Islamists within the Arab world and outside it.[21] It reflects an *idée fixe* in the ideology of political Islam and is completely contrary to history, the present day and logic. The West is not a monolith, physically or politically. Indeed, public opinion in the West is often opposed to Western governments' policies: the demonstrations against the 2003 invasion of Iraq that swept across Western capitals were much larger than any in the Arab world.[22] Moreover, Western governments are not interested in Islam or in any other religion, especially; their real focus lies in advancing their own economic interests.[23] Western states have often formed alliances with hard-line Islamist governments and groups because it has served their interests to do so: the US supported the regimes of General Zia-ul-Haq (1924–1988) in Pakistan and the Muslim Brotherhood in Egypt.[24] The US also funded the Taliban movement in its formative stage,[25] in addition to the fact that the movement's closest ally for decades has been the Saudi government, which is the mouthpiece of Sunni Islam. The Islamists completely ignore all these facts because the West's hostility is one of the greatest motivational concepts in their drive to mobilise young people to participate in the *jihad* to establish a caliphate.

As demonstrated earlier, the essence of political Islam is the religious struggle in which it only sees the world as a battleground between Muslims and non-believers. Therefore it must keep the flame of hatred for the West burning or else it loses its *raison d'être*. Islamists ignore, or deny, any human vision that calls for tolerance among humankind – when, for example, a ship sets sail from Europe to break the Israeli blockade of the Palestinians in Gaza we discover that among those showing solidarity with Gaza are not only those who are Jewish but one of whom is a Holocaust survivor.[26] However, this means very little to the Islamists because hatred for Jews is embedded in political Islam. When rabbis demonstrate in front of Trump Tower in New York in protest at his decree preventing Muslims from entering the US, the Islamist sites do not publish a word about it. When the German chancellor, Angela Merkel, relaxed immigration controls to allow hundreds of thousands of Syrian Muslim migrants into Germany in 2015, Islamist sites not only failed to acknowledge this as an act of humanity but wrote this off as Germany's need for cheap labour.[27] Some even accused her of carrying out a plot to convert the Muslims to Christianity.[28]

A Muslim is taught love and tolerance, but an Islamist's

political ideology is based on a hatred of non-Muslims, on contempt for them and on a distrust of their intentions. Hostility to the West is one of the most important pre-disposing factors for Islamist terrorism and is the fuel that the machine of political Islam needs in order to remain in operation. Here we discover again that terrorism and dictatorship stem from the same source: dictators, as we have seen, all need a conspiracy theory in order to garner militant followers and to wage war against real or imaginary enemies.

A feeling of inferiority and humiliation

Khaled al-Berry was born in 1972 to a lower-middle-class family in the city of Assiut in Upper Egypt. While still in secondary school, he joined the Jama'a Islamiya (an Islamist group that has carried out many terrorist operations in Egypt). Al-Berry worked his way up within the organisation until he was responsible for its activities in secondary schools in the whole Assiut Governorate. He remained a leading member of the organisation throughout his studies at the Assiut College of Medicine, but after thinking things over for a long while he left the organisation and abandoned the Islamist group's way of thinking. Al-Berry did not practise medicine but pursued his love of writing, became a well-known author and now lives in London.

Al-Berry recorded his experiences in a 2006 book entitled *Life is More Beautiful than Paradise*,[29] in which it becomes clear that a feeling of inferiority was one of the most important motives for his joining the Islamist group. This bright and industrious young man could not find a place for his talent in the class-ridden society of Upper Egypt due to his social status. Even when he was a child, he had been asked to leave the house of a friend whose father was a university professor, and hence middle class, and his final school examinations were marked down by a teacher who gave top marks to a lower-scoring boy whose father was a man of some influence. His resulting feeling of inferiority was replaced by one of authority, handed to him by the Islamist group. Very soon, the socially marginal young man became a powerful figure in the city and personally supervised the separation of boys and girls at the College of Medicine as well as taking part in punishing a Copt for denigrating Islam.

Al-Berry describes how he came to this point: "The idea that I'd formed early on [was that] the Islamist movement was a movement of the resentful middle class."[30] Elsewhere he writes, "The Jama'a Islamiya had opened up new horizons for me in my rebellion against the typical petit bourgeois upbringing that I had received at home and at school and caused me to submerge myself in the life of different social classes as a natural outcome of missionary work. This placed me in an independent category that neither belonged to any of these classes nor ought to do so."[31] And further on, he adds:

With all due respect to the many studies that point to the economic element as a factor in the phenomenon of the Jama'a Islamiya, offering as evidence statistics on the number of committed members of the Islamist movement vis-à-vis their educational and social backgrounds, I believe that these studies fail to take into account the divide between the Jamaʻaʼs leadership hierarchy and the vast mass of its adherents. The primary motor of the Jamaʻaʼs work consists almost entirely of university graduates. I try so far as is possible to avoid theorizing, but what I felt when a committed member of the Jamaʻa and remain convinced of to this day is that political Islam is a reflection of the crisis of the middle class in societies in which this class, and those below it, have lost their faith in social mobility as a key to future opportunities.[32]

A feeling of inferiority, social injustice and a sense of hopelessness about professional advancement are thus all predisposing factors for terrorism. Some people may have reservations about this claim because some of those who carry out terrorist acts are Western citizens, born and raised in Western countries. Any reservations will disappear straight away if one visits Molenbeek in Brussels, for example, or an immigrant district in Paris or in any European city. The first-generation Arab immigrants were drawn to France in the 1960s to do the menial, manual jobs that French people would not do, such as domestic work and cleaning. These first Arab immigrants recognised their lowly position *vis-à-vis* the French, but their ultimate ambition was to work hard and keep their French employers happy. However, their children have been born in France and have had a French education. As they grew up, they discovered that the France they belong to still treats them as it did their parents, as second-class citizens, and that French society recognises their rights in theory but dismisses them in practice. Many members of this young generation thus live in 'ghettos' and feel as inferior and as resentful towards their society as the Egyptian graduates about whom al-Berry wrote. To all intents and purposes, they are part of the developing world in spite of them 'theoretically' living in France.

Added to this feeling of inferiority is the humiliation that Islamists undergo in prison as a result of torture and inhumane treatment. The constant feature here is that many leaders of terrorist movements in prison have undergone torture more horrific than a Western citizen could imagine.[33] If you are arrested on a charge of terrorism in many Arab countries, you will know that the torture will not be limited to you alone but will take in your family members and possibly your friends. Your mother, sister or spouse may be sexually abused in front of your eyes to make you confess to whatever the officer wants you to. A desire to avenge the humiliation meted out to you is a predisposing factor for terrorism. Here again, we can see clearly the parallel with the serious damage wrought by dictatorship, with feelings of inferiority, social injustice, oppression and the violation of human rights all being the usual features of any dictatorship.

The continued existence of these predisposing factors for terrorism within authoritarian states are among the worst symptoms of the dictatorship syndrome.

8

The course of the syndrome

Susceptible peoples

Does the dictatorship syndrome affect some peoples and not others?

We must be careful that we do not unwittingly apply prejudices, as all human beings are equal in their capabilities and rights. Everyone also has the right to justice, but the concept of how to carry out that justice differs from one country to the next. Countries that lack a democratic tradition put up less resistance to dictatorship, and countries under the thumbs of men of religion are more receptive to dictatorship.[1] The Iranians, for example, resisted the corrupt and bloody regime of Shah Mohammad Reza Pahlavi (1919–1980), but their resistance for the most part bore a religious overtone under their spiritual guide, Ayatollah Khomeini. When the revolution succeeded and the Shah was deposed in 1979, Khomeini returned from exile, formed a government and stated clearly that it was the government of God and anyone who disobeyed would be going against God.[2] None of his followers objected to this concept because Khomeini had total control over the lives of most Iranians in the name of religion, and his combination of political and religious authority was even welcome after the excesses of the Shah.

Another factor contributes to people's receptivity to dictatorship and that is the absence of the notion of the state in their consciousness.[3] People whose cultural tradition is tribal are less likely to resist authoritarianism. The member states of the Arab Gulf Cooperation Council are Saudi Arabia, Oman, the United Arab Emirates, Kuwait, Qatar and Bahrain, and they have all been run by royal families for decades. There have always been disputes between members of the royal families over power: in 1896 in Kuwait, Shaykh Mubarak al-Sabah (1840–1915) reportedly took power by killing his half-brothers, Muhammad and Jarrah;[4] while in Qatar in 1995, Shaykh Hamad bin Khalifa Al Thani (b. 1952) seized control from his father with the support of the army.[5] From time to time, disturbances arise for religious and sectarian reasons between the Shiʿa and Sunnis, or between some hard-line shaykhs and the government. These rumblings are generally put down immediately with the utmost force. Aside from this, the citizens of the Gulf states generally appear satisfied with their rulers. Of course, this is helped by the rise in the level of individual income as a result of proceeds from the sale of oil,[6] but the most important reason for this complacency is the long shadow cast by a tribal culture.

The Gulf citizen does not consider their ruler to be a constitutional monarch or a head of state in the democratic meaning of the term, which would see him subject to an election process or some form of accountability. In the eyes of his citizens, the ruler of any Gulf state is the shaykh of the supreme tribe, a family elder, with the traditions and duties of honour imposing on the younger family members obedience and reverence for him as the symbol of the tribe.

He is the wise, caring, considerate and firm patriarch all rolled into one. In governments of the Gulf states, parliaments and political parties are all essentially clients of the patriarch. There are other political parties in opposition, but they are merely symbolic, not democratic, as the king is above everyone else – the de facto sole ruler who decides, by his will alone, all the domestic and external policies of the state. The status of the king (along with most members of the royal family) is above any sort of accountability such that directing any criticism toward the ruling family is considered a crime and can lead to many years in prison.[7] There is also no separation between the state budget and the expenses of the ruling family, and this in itself is considered taboo. The state is the state of the king, the land is his and the people are his obedient sons and daughters. Of course, this arrangement is not exclusive to Gulf states; in Brunei, a *lèse-majesté* law – which criminalises criticism of the royal family – is strictly enforced.

When the Egyptian revolution of 2011 succeeded in removing Hosni Mubarak from power, the Gulf rulers were greatly perturbed and came out on the side of the deposed president.[8] They saw what had happened as evidence of the ingratitude of the Egyptians who had mistreated their father Mubarak instead of according him due reverence and obedience. A member of the military council that took power after the Egyptian revolution even alleged that Saudi Arabia had offered millions of dollars to the council to prevent Mubarak being tried publicly, but the military council – under pressure given the mass demonstrations – allowed the public trial to go ahead. Why would Saudi Arabia offer mouth-watering sums to prevent the public trial of a deposed dictator? This transcends any loyalty from the Saudi king, Abdullah bin Abdulaziz Al Saud (1924–2015), for Mubarak. Egypt is the most populous Arab state[9] and has had great influence in the Arab world, and the sight of Mubarak standing behind bars, like any common criminal, doubtless had the potential to change the political consciousness of the people of Saudi Arabia and the Gulf states. Citizens there might start to think that their ruler, too, was not the father of the nation, not the shaykh of the tribe and not the symbol of the nation, but that on reflection he was an ordinary official who could be held to account, tried and sentenced for any crimes he might have committed. The Gulf rulers considered this a real danger to their thrones, and they did everything within their power to impede the Egyptian revolution and to prevent it realising its aims.[10]

In non-democratic states, it is feasible for a dictator to remain in power for a long time, but is it the case elsewhere that democratic traditions prevent the emergence of a dictatorship? The answer to that is yes – but not always. Even in democratic states, the people might live through periods of defeat, loss of self-confidence, upheaval and chaos, and at those times a sense of humiliation or fear of the unknown can cause them to look for a strong leader who can protect them and restore their lost dignity and security in exchange for loyalty and total submission. The defeat of Germany in the First World War, its demeaning treatment in the Treaty of Versailles in 1919, the imposition of eye-watering reparations, the Great Depression and the loss of faith in German nationalism were all factors that led to the Germans welcoming the National Socialist movement and being dazzled by the leadership of Adolf Hitler.

The same applies to Italy, where the loss of state cohesion and prestige after the First World War, the suffocating economic crisis, the spread of poverty and unemployment, the disturbances such as food riots, which paralysed the state, and the attempts by workers to take over factories by force were all harbingers of Italy's descent into total chaos.[11] They struck fear into the hearts of Italians and made them welcome Benito Mussolini, the leader of the fascist movement, as the strongman capable of restoring law and order.

This reaction is akin to that of a group of people in a locked room when a fire breaks out. The fire comes at them from all directions and they do not know what to do to save themselves from burning to death, and then behold: a strong person appears, assumes command and starts giving orders. The others all submit to him immediately so that he can bring about their rescue. We must also sadly recognise that most people are not against dictatorship as a matter of principle but only reject it if it turns out badly and harms their personal interests, as in the case of the 'good citizen' we met earlier. If people's lives take a turn for the better in the shade of authoritarianism, if employment opportunities increase by reasonable degrees, if education and health services are available at no or low cost, and if the authorities only oppress others, then most people will give their support to a dictator. History teaches us that those who consider freedom more important than anything else are generally a minority of the population, whereas the majority of citizens consider the ability to earn a livelihood much more important than freedom.

In 1884, José de la Cruz Porfirio Díaz Mori (1830–1915) took power in Mexico and convened a cabinet meeting. I imagine Díaz holding up a loaf of bread in his left hand and in his right a club as he declares, "This is my system of governance: I shall give bread to all citizens, but if anyone demands more than bread I shall bludgeon him on the head with this club."[12] Whether or not he actually said these words, this principle sustained him in power for 27 years and gave rise to the common expression: '*pan o palo*' (bread or the bludgeon). Díaz's blunt alternatives were to be copied by Hitler, Saddam Hussein, António de Oliveira Salazar, Gamal Abdel Nasser and many other dictators who similarly worked on improving the living standards of the masses at the same time as mercilessly crushing any political opposition. This has always led to the establishment of authoritarian rule, with people only rising up against the dictator when driven by hunger.[13]

The formation of the dictator

There is a trend among psychologists who have studied the lives of dictators to draw a connection between the violence practised by a dictator and the grief and pain suffered by him in his childhood.[14] The prevalence of this suffering seems too overwhelming to be coincidental.

Saddam Hussein, for example, had an extremely hard childhood. His father died before he was born, and his mother married a man who mistreated him so badly that he fled the family home to complete his education. Nasser's childhood was also not a happy one. His mother died when he was eight years old, and he described the effect that had on him: "My mother's death was a tragic event in itself, but losing her this way was a shock so deep that time failed to remedy [it]."[15] Hitler was a wretched child due to the severity of his father's beatings, and the Egyptian dictator Abdel Fattah el-Sisi stated in a press conference, "When I was a child, people used to beat me up. What would I say to them, eh? Tomorrow I'll be a big guy and beat them up."[16]

The Serbian president Slobodan Milošević (1941–2006), responsible for the genocide during the Bosnian war, did not have a 'normal' childhood either. He was born when his country was under Nazi rule, and his father – who had separated from his mother after the Second World War – committed suicide in 1962, a great scandal. Milošević was brought up by his mother, a teacher and hard-line communist with an authoritarian and violent character. He never once mentioned his father and kept the fact of his suicide pent up inside him. When he reached his thirties, his mother also committed suicide and that, too, took an enormous psychological toll on him.[17]

The psychologist Alice Miller undertook research into the childhood of dictators and presented her findings in a lecture in New York City in 1998. She stated:

[It] didn't surprise me that in the childhood of people who later became dictators, I have always found a nightmarish horror, a record of continued lies and humiliations, which, upon the attainment of adulthood, impelled them to acts of merciless revenge on society … In the lives of all the tyrants I analysed, I also found without exception paranoid trains of thought bound up with their biographies in early childhood and the repression of the experiences they had been through.[18]

A dictator's thirst for power, his tendency to employ strong-arm tactics and his use of violence to rule others are all traits that appear early on in his character. During the annual celebrations for the El-Nahda School in the Cairo district of al-Zaher, the 17-year-old Nasser acted the role of Julius Caesar and found that he liked the emotions he felt during the performance, as he stated later on in his press conferences.[19] This perhaps makes sense given that the young Nasser chose to read mostly biographies of strongmen and leaders. The only novel he spoke about with enduring admiration was *The Return of the Spirit* (1933) by the Egyptian author Tawfiq al-Hakim, which described the Egyptian people as a storehouse of enormous cultural energy built up over long centuries, a people just waiting for a leader to adore and believe in.[20] At that point, they would as one fall under the leadership of a strongman who would lead Egypt back to its rightful place at the forefront of civilisation.

As for the young Hitler, his preferred readings reflected his belligerent personality, "His favorite game to play outside was cowboys and Indians. Tales of the American West were very popular among boys in Austria and Germany. Books by James Fenimore Cooper and especially German writer Karl May were eagerly read and re-enacted. May, who had never been to America, invented a hero named Old Shatterhand, a white man who always won his battles with Native Americans, defeating his enemies through sheer will power and bravery. Young Hitler read and re-read every one of May's books about Old Shatterhand, totaling more than 70 novels."[21]

Certain traits also appeared early on in Mussolini, who reportedly "gained a reputation for bullying and fighting during his childhood."[22] Even at the young age of ten, "he was expelled from a religious boarding school for stabbing a classmate in the hand, and another stabbing incident took place at his next school. He also admitted to knifing a girlfriend in the arm. Meanwhile, he purportedly pinched people at church to make them cry, led gangs of boys on raids of local farmsteads and eventually became adept at dueling with swords."[23]

When looking at photographs of a dictator as a schoolchild or student, it has often struck me that he will appear different from his peers – quiet, isolated, enigmatic and gloomy, as if hiding some secret or waiting for something to happen that no one else knows about. In his youth, a dictator looks like an actor huddled in the wings of a theatre, waiting for his cue to appear on stage: the moment of his coming to power.

With few exceptions, such as Salazar and François Duvalier 'Papa Doc' (1907–1971) of Haiti, dictators rarely devote their efforts to furthering their own education. The reason for this is not any lack of ability on the part of the dictator, but rather a lack of patience when it comes to arduous study that might, under propitious circumstances, give him a good skill or the opportunity to change his life for the better.* It is, after all, not *his life* he wants to change, but *the world*. He wants to destroy the reality in his own country and rebuild it, and he can only do that by seizing power. Nothing fascinates a dictator as much as finding a way to seize power, and for this he will always use networks to his

---

* Gamal Abdel Nasser and Saddam Hussein both attended law school for a time and dropped out to enlist in the army.

advantage, for example by organising secret cells or joining the army. A dictator's life starts the second he attains power and, from that moment, he passes through three stages: accumulating sole power, glory and supreme isolation.

The quest for sole power

In 1968, after the coup organised by the Ba'ath Party in Iraq succeeded in taking power, Ahmed Hassan al-Bakr (1914–1982) took on the job of president of the republic. The name of Saddam Hussein came to the fore as someone who played a notable role in the coup, and he was promoted through the ranks until he became vice president. Then, in 1979, President al-Bakr convened a meeting with the party leadership and announced that he was unwell from all the responsibility of being president, wanted to retire and rest, and was appointing his colleague Saddam Hussein to succeed him. It is not hard to imagine that al-Bakr's resignation was not of his own doing. Rather, it is commonly believed that al-Bakr had been forced into his retirement by Saddam Hussein, who had gained the loyalty of the army and then demanded that the 65-year-old president hand power over to him in a calm and dignified manner rather than having it snatched from him by force.[24] In this way, Saddam Hussein was planning to concentrate all power in his own hands. However, the reactions from the Ba'ath leadership were not as he expected, and many of them opposed President al-Bakr's resignation.[25] They claimed that al-Bakr was still in good enough health to be able to run the affairs of state and that 'Comrade Hussein' needed a great deal of time before he would be ready to assume the presidency. But these objections had no effect. Al-Bakr insisted on resigning, and a decree accepting his resignation was ratified, along with a second decree appointing Saddam Hussein as the president of the Republic of Iraq on 16 July 1979.

Saddam Hussein retained the names of those who had opposed his appointment, and a few days later on 22 July 1979 he convened an enlarged assembly of the Ba'ath Party leadership during which he stated that he had uncovered a great conspiracy against the party.[26] He called upon a member of the party who confessed to being a member of a secret cell of conspirators who had been planning a coup in Iraq in favour of Hafez al-Assad (then president of Syria). Saddam Hussein took the microphone and stated that anyone who heard his name called out must stand up, repeat the party slogan and leave the hall immediately.[27]

Deep silence prevailed, and those present were struck with fear that their names could be on the list. Saddam Hussein read out the names of the conspirators one by one, and they were naturally those who had opposed his appointment.[28] All the 'conspirators' were arrested on the spot by the military police and, when Saddam Hussein finished reading out the names, he declared, "And now we have put an end to the traitors. Is the Ba'ath Party not sufficient for all the noble and devoted members in this hall?"[29]

Loud applause rang out, and those present seemed to breathe a sigh of relief at having been saved. Saddam Hussein then spoke about how great the party and the 1968 coup were, and stated, "If those conspirators had political demands, we would have listened and discussed them with them. By God Almighty, had they asked for power, we would have given it to them and wished them every success, but they plotted against us and betrayed us. Why did they stab us in the back?"[30]

Saddam Hussein's voice was shaking with emotion. He took out his handkerchief to wipe away his tears. Many of those present were also crying audibly as they all shouted out, "We will sacrifice our spirit and our blood for you, *Abu Uday*!"[31]

One of those present asked to speak and stated, "Everything that the leadership has done is correct, and everything that you are going to do will also be correct, but conspiracies will never end while the traitors are still alive."[32]

Speaker after speaker restated this, with them all demanding instant death for the conspirators, criminal traitors who did not deserve to breathe the air of the great country of Iraq. Saddam Hussein reassured those present that in cases of treachery he would act with the sword. Indeed, the conspirators were swiftly put on trial with reportedly 31 incarcerated (many of whom were to die in prison) and 20 sentenced to death. This violent consolidation of power became known in Arabic as the 'Paradise Hall Massacre', after the hall in which Saddam Hussein made his statement.

The method of execution, however, was quite unique. Often, Saddam Hussein would force members of the Ba'ath Party themselves to execute their condemned colleagues.[33] The following scene was repeated at such executions. The condemned man was shackled and blindfolded. He was on his feet, and in front of him would stand a member of the Ba'ath Party with a revolver in his hand. Behind the Ba'ath Party member stood a soldier with his rifle aimed at the two men. The soldier would order the party member to shoot his colleague and, if he hesitated or refused, the soldier would shoot them both dead.[34] In this way, Ba'ath Party members participated in murdering their colleagues.

By carrying out executions in this manner, Saddam Hussein realised a number of objectives: the act of killing could not be pinned on one individual, making it difficult for relatives of the victim to demand revenge. Second, this showed up the members of the party whose loyalty was deficient or who were unable to kill their colleagues. No one dared refuse, but some had a nervous breakdown and others fired away from the victim, leaving the attendant soldier to carry out the execution himself. However the most important objective of this method of slaughter was to signal to those concerned that Saddam Hussein had become the sole ruler of Iraq and that, as the source of all power, he was going to rid himself not only of his political rivals but also of anyone who did not offer their total submission. The statement spoken by that Ba'ath Party member was exactly what Saddam Hussein wanted to hear from everyone: "Everything that the leadership has done is correct, and everything that you are going to do will also be correct."

Every dictator, without exception, has acted like Saddam Hussein. The moment a dictator achieves power, he embarks on a struggle to concentrate power solely in his hands.

In Egypt in the late 1940s, Nasser, along with a group of other young army officers, formed the secret organisation the 'Free Officers'. Together, they distributed anti-monarchical pamphlets and held secret meetings to plan a military putsch. The Free Officers were joined by a senior army officer with the rank of general, Muhammad Naguib,[35] who had a reputation as an efficient leader who was both brave and patriotic. In fact, many officers joined the organisation out of loyalty to General Naguib. On 23 July 1952, the Free Officers carried out their coup and took power. A few months later the monarchy was abolished, and on 18 June 1953 a republic was declared with Naguib as the first republican president in the history of Egypt.

Nasser soon became irritated by Naguib's broad popularity in Egypt and Sudan (as the latter came from an Egyptian–Sudanese family) as well as his public demands for the army's return to barracks and the creation of a real democracy.* In 1954, Nasser made the decision to arrest Naguib, now major-general, remove him from his post and place him under house arrest for the following 16 years of Nasser's rule (1954–1970). Nasser went on to remove many of his comrades in various ways, although when he tried to oust Abdel Hakim Amer, commander-in-chief of the army, Amer resisted with force. He enjoyed great popularity among the officers, and the threat of a split in the army prevented Nasser from sacking him more than once.[36]

After the defeat of 1967, when Israel occupied Sinai, Gaza, the Golan Heights, East Jerusalem and the West Bank, Nasser's declaration of resignation was followed, as you will remember, by the masses demanding he stay in power. A few weeks later on 14 September 1967, a communiqué was issued announcing the suicide of Amer in a mysterious incident and under strange circumstances.[37]

---

* The 'coup' was initially presented as a 'movement of the army' with the stated goal of the Free Officers in 1952 to retain power for three years during which time a constitutional government would be established.

To this day, Amer's family insist that they have convincing evidence that points to Nasser's involvement in his death.[38]

That moment of absolute power is the moment that every dictator strives for, and he finds no peace of mind until he achieves it. "To be thus is nothing, but to be safely thus," as Shakespeare's Macbeth says. This overheated quest for sole power seems to be a psychological phenomenon more than a political or objective one. A dictator often removes people who constitute no threat to him but with whom he cannot bring himself to share power – even if they are one of his closest comrades.[39]

Does a dictator feel pangs of conscience when he kills off his friends? The answer is not easy to ascertain. A few years ago, a study compiled by psychologists for the US CIA was made public. It comprised psychological profiles of some of the world's dictators.[40] In the section on Saddam Hussein, the report states the following:

The labels 'madman of the Middle East' and 'megalomaniac' are often affixed to Saddam, but in fact there is no evidence that he is suffering from a psychotic disorder.

Saddam's pursuit of power for himself and Iraq is boundless. In fact, in his mind, the destiny of Saddam and Iraq are one and indistinguishable ... In pursuit of his messianic dreams, there is no evidence he is constrained by conscience; his only loyalty is to Saddam Hussein. In pursuing his goals, Saddam uses aggression instrumentally. He uses whatever force is necessary, and will, if he deems it expedient, go to extremes of violence, including the use of weapons of mass destruction ...

While Hussein is not psychotic, he has a strong

paranoid orientation … Saddam has no wish to be a martyr, and survival is his number one priority. A self-proclaimed revolutionary pragmatist, he does not wish a conflict in which Iraq will be grievously damaged and his stature as a leader destroyed … Saddam will not go down to the last flaming bunker if he has a way out, but he can be extremely dangerous and will stop at nothing if he is backed into a corner.[41]

What this profile points out most significantly is that the fate of Saddam Hussein and that of Iraq were bound together as one. This notion is common to all dictators, and they mostly express it implicitly in their speeches and at press conferences. There have, however, been some, such as Idi Amin (1925–2003) in Uganda and Muammar Gaddafi, who have exemplified it.

This identification of the state with the dictator leads unavoidably to a number of results.

First, there can be no space for any delegation of authority, as the strongman is the state and his downfall would mean the downfall of the nation. In his last press conference before he fell, for example, Mubarak is reported to have stated, "Egyptians need to choose… either me, or chaos."[42]

Second, any criticism of the strongman will be seen as defaming the state because the strongman is the state. For that reason, a dictator will consider any opposition to be treachery carried out by agents of foreign security organisations whose aim is to destroy the country and foment chaos.[43]

Third, he will not see that disposing of his opponents or rivals has anything to do with a power struggle. It is just something the strongman has to do because the call of the state is more important than friendship, love or family relationships.

History gives us a clear example of how family relationships come second to the state. On 16 July 1941, as fierce battles raged between the Nazi and Soviet armies, Stalin's oldest son, Yakov, was taken prisoner by the Nazis. The Nazi High Command later offered to exchange him for a German field marshal, Friedrich von Paulus, who'd been captured by the Soviets at Stalingrad (1942–1943). However, legend has it that Stalin turned this offer down in a terse letter in which he wrote, "You have in your hands not only my son Yakov but millions of my sons. Either you free them all or my son will share their fate."[44]

The story goes that, a few days after Stalin's letter of refusal, Yakov tried to escape from the prison and was shot dead by Nazi guards. This is the Nazi version of how Yakov died, but it is not accepted by many who believe that the Nazis killed him deliberately. When Stalin rejected the Nazi's exchange offer, was he not aware that he was putting his son's life in danger? He must have been, but he opted for duty over saving his son.

This justification of 'doing one's duty' has been used in other power struggles when a dictator considers that in ridding himself of his rivals he is acting out of obligation. A dictator believes that he embodies the will of the nation and can do nothing else.[45] This false belief in duty, which leads a dictator to commit crimes, explains not only a dictator's lack of feelings of regret but also his occasional empathy with the victims he has just had liquidated: a dictator may feel sad for his victim because he believes that ridding himself of them is necessary to save the nation, but that he is above all others and that he cannot allow human emotion to be an impediment.[46] He believes that giving the order to kill his colleagues does not, at that moment, represent his personal wish but the will of the nation or the revolution. After the crime has been carried out, the scene is like that of a dictator inspecting the field after battle only to find the bodies of his colleagues; at this point he might sincerely mourn their loss.

In 1896, after Shaykh Mubarak killed his two brothers in order to ascend the throne, he summoned the Kuwaiti elders to a meeting, informed them of the death of his brothers and, according to some accounts, burst into tears.[47] Mubarak considered the death of his brothers a matter of national importance for the establishment of the state of Kuwait, but after their death he mourned them – in the same way as Nasser considered that ridding himself of Amer after the 1967 defeat was a national duty for the salvation of Egypt. The truth of the matter is that Nasser wanted to save his regime but, as he had identified himself as the nation, the salvation of his regime meant the salvation of Egypt. After Amer's 'disappearance', Nasser continued to describe him as one of his closest friends and mourned his loss, reportedly visibly holding back tears whenever he was mentioned.

The same paradoxical behaviour was displayed by Saddam Hussein after Dr Riyyad Ibrahim al-Hajj, his personal doctor and friend for over 25 years, was killed on his instruction. The doctor died during horrendous torture at the hands of Saddam Hussein's secret service agents. The Iraqi dictator then summoned the doctor's family to come and meet him, and he cried tears of sorrow in front of them.[48]

But even once a dictator has garnered all power to himself and his will has become the dominant factor in governing the nation, the people and the state, there may appear from time to time some person courageous enough to confront him.

In November 1979, the twelfth annual congress of the Romanian Communist Party was convened to re-elect Nicolae Ceauşescu as president of the republic. Ceauşescu had been named the general secretary of the party in 1965 and had been president of the republic since 1974. He was the sole ruler of Romania and as a consequence his re-election should have been a rubber-stamping exercise. Speaker after speaker thus spoke in praise of Comrade Ceauşescu, the great leader of the party and the state. Suddenly a party member, Constantin Pîrvulescu, asked to speak and declared his opposition to Ceauşescu's re-election. The congress hall fell silent and then other party members started to boo him. Pîrvulescu responded by telling them, "Shame on you hypocrites."[49]

Pîrvulescu was removed from the microphone, ejected from the congress hall and, as the dissident was 84 at the time, Ceauşescu felt it sufficient to have him sacked from his position, stripped of his party membership and placed under house arrest.[50]

Another brave act of confrontation took place in Egypt. After the defeat of 1967, and as a sop to the popular anger expressed in student and worker demonstrations against the regime,[51] Nasser decided to reform the ruling party (the Arab Socialist Union) from the bottom up by holding elections.[52] No one knows what drove Shaykh 'Ashur to stand for election – he was an obscure cleric and the imam of a small mosque in Alexandria. Whatever the reason, he stood and was elected in 1969 as one of the 2,000 party members who made up the general congress of the party. During the first session, he found himself in front of Nasser in a meeting attended by the president's deputies, cabinet and top brass and being broadcast live by all radio and television stations.[53] Shaykh 'Ashur asked for permission to address the meeting. He then stood up to voice his objections to what he considered the gap between word and action, between slogan and reality. He stated that government officials were always going on about socialism and were forever demanding citizens to accept austerity and to reduce their consumerism, but at the same time they were spending shameless amounts themselves, leading lives of affluence and driving around in the most expensive cars.[54] Then the Shaykh addressed Nasser, "We elected you as president of the republic, not as our master."[55]

Shaykh 'Ashur disappeared after that and was never heard from again,[56] but it would seem that most Egyptians liked what he had said. The revolutionary poet Ahmed Fouad Negm even praised him in a short poem in the colloquial language:

O my country, a great hurrah!
For Shaykh 'Ashur, with the heart of a lion!
Hurrah for a real son of the country!
Were there eleven more of you,
none of this would have happened!

You, my country, would be so different!
Hurrah for Shaykh 'Ashur. Hurrah![57]

In the Egyptian dialect, the expression 'behind the sun' is used for someone who has completely disappeared and whose whereabouts no one knows. After Shaykh 'Ashur confronted Nasser, the following joke became popular in Egypt: the Russian astronaut Yuri Gagarin set off on a trip to space. As he was passing the sun, he noticed someone behind it, calling out to him, "Gagarin, Gagarin. Peace and greetings upon you!"

Gagarin asked him, "Who are you?"

And he received the response, "I'm Shaykh 'Ashur. Abdel Nasser has chucked me behind the sun."[58]

This absolute power, being vested in him alone, is what drives a dictator on to the second step, the stage of glory.

A lust for glory

These initiatives on the part of some brave individuals have no effect on the course of history, despite the noble intentions of those who carry them out – mere bubbles that appear on the surface from time to time. Rather, a dictator who has consolidated power in his hands will quickly go about setting up the machinery to administer his power.

This machinery works efficiently and systematically on its own, without the dictator having to give instructions. It is a complex machine and takes in thousands of people. Police officers, liberally dosed with money and privileges, defend the regime by torturing and killing in the knowledge that they have complete immunity from accountability.

Army generals themselves form a wealthy class, ready as they are to kill any number of people to preserve their privileges. Corrupt judges are directed by security officers as to the rulings they should issue in various cases. Members of the ruling party are trained in hypocrisy and opportunism so they can snatch every chance to enrich themselves by dint of their party membership. A whole array of journalists, broadcasters and media moguls who support the strongman and never miss an opportunity to praise his greatness and intelligence are undoubtedly at the beck and call of the security services; they are willing to report on their colleagues or even satisfy the sexual needs of high-ranking state officials in exchange for the untold riches they make in protecting the regime.[59]

Atop this giant pyramid of power sits a dictator whose overbearing will is beyond question and discussion. Notwithstanding the thousands of articles, conferences, seminars, presentations by committees and speeches made by politicians, the sole authority in the country is the strongman alone, and – as absolute power corrupts absolutely – a dictator generally amasses huge amounts of money for himself[60] and his children by siphoning off state funds or by manipulating people. However, the greatest reward for a dictator is not money but glory, and the lust for glory in the psyche of a dictator runs far deeper than any ordinary person's libido.

This *idée fixe*, the lust for glory, explains much of a dictator's behaviour that may appear exceptionally odd to us. What else could drive Ceaușescu to build the second largest administrative building in the world in a developing country like Romania? The building is so huge that the

present Romanian government, with all its various admin-
istrations, departments and employees, can only find use
for 30 per cent of its rooms.[61] In 1976, having been sole
ruler of the Central African Republic for ten years and a
fan of Napoleon Bonaparte, General Bokassa decided to
bestow upon himself the title of 'Emperor'.[62] He commis-
sioned French experts (naturally on exorbitant salaries) to
make his imperial inauguration match Napoleon's. Everything was imported from France, from horses and wine
to the emperor's gold crown studded with diamonds.[63] A
crown was also made for the empress, Catherine Dengui-
adé, the youngest of Bokassa's 19 wives.[64] For this one-day
coronation ceremony, Bokassa is estimated to have spent a
third of the state budget at a time when the Central African
population was literally starving.[65] Bokassa's lust for glory
had got the better of his capacity to think or to consider the
consequences of his actions.

It was a lust for glory, too, that brought Gaddafi, the dicta-
tor of Libya, to proclaim his many titles, including: Colonel,
Leader, Leader of the Libyan Revolution, Custodian of Arab
Nationalism, Dean of Arab Rulers, Head of the African
Union, King of Kings of Africa, Commander of the Tuareg,
Leader of the Association of Coastal and Desert States, Leader
of the Popular Islamic Leadership and Imam of the Muslims.

In the case of the Ugandan dictator Idi Amin, his official title listed the awards – many somewhat bizarre – that
he had bestowed upon himself: President for Life, Field
Marshal, Victoria Cross, Distinguished Service Order, Military Cross, Lord of All the Beasts of the Earth and Fishes
of the Seas and Conqueror of the British Empire in Africa
in General and Uganda in Particular.[66]

Such self-aggrandisement is not restricted to epithets. Often, public squares have a statue or an enormous image of the dictator,[67] and all sorts of other things are named after him. No dictator in modern history has failed to institute a 'mega-project' to make his name live on and to deliver him a feeling of glory. There have been Gaddafi's 'Great Man-Made River' project (1984), Mubarak's Toshka Project (1997), the High Dam Project of Gamal Abdel Nasser (1960, inaugurated a decade later) and el-Sisi's Suez Canal Corridor Area Project (2014/5) for which el-Sisi spent 64 billion Egyptian pounds (approximately 6 billion British pounds in today's money) to widen the Suez Canal. It quickly became clear that the project would not generate any profit because a proper feasibility study had not been carried out,[68] but that in no way dampened el-Sisi's enthusiasm and he clearly had spectacular plans for the opening ceremony. On the day itself, el-Sisi stood in full dress uniform adorned with his orders, decorations and medals, smiling among the heads of state who had come to congratulate him.[69] Children presented him with bouquets of flowers, flocks of doves flew overhead and cannons were fired in salute. It would appear that this glory-satisfying spectacle was, for el-Sisi, more important than the economic reality in any form.

It was the same lust for glory that drove General Rafael Trujillo (1891–1961), who ruled the Dominican Republic for 31 years (1930–1961), to order churches to erect signs that read, *"Dios en cielo, Trujillo en tierra"* (God in Heaven, Trujillo on Earth). Trujillo did not stop at glory for himself but extended it to his children, making his four-year-old son a colonel in the army.[70] Saparmurat Niyazov (1940–2006), the dictator of Turkmenistan, similarly sought religious glory. He wrote a two-volume book of spiritual-moral guidance called the *Ruhnama* (*Book of the Soul*) (2001, 2004) and ordered it to be studied in mosques alongside the Qur'an.

Glory is an inevitable stage in a dictator's journey and so it, too, inevitably leads to the final stage, that of supreme isolation.

Supreme isolation

Supreme isolation is the inescapable destiny of a dictator. This means not only that he is cut off from reality but also that a virtual world has sprung up around him that operates in parallel to daily life.[71] This is a world in which a dictator can enjoy unbridled power, imagine himself as he would like himself to be and in which he hears what he wishes to hear, conjuring up for himself achievements, acts of heroism and victories – all figments of his imagination and unconnected to real events. The machinery of oppression crushes his opponents and rivals and mercilessly grinds down anyone who does not believe in his virtual world or who questions it.

A dictator's sensitivity to any criticism and his fury at anyone who criticises him are due not solely to his megalomania but also to his fear of any scratch on the surface of his virtual world. He will do anything to hold on to his belief that he is a great leader, an exception among all in existence, and an inspired man who has saved his nation from loss and whose courage and genius have brought about its renaissance. A dictator's fury at anyone who doubts his virtual world is like the wrath of a fundamentalist when someone questions his religion: a mixture of resentment, hysterical animosity and a fear of a loss of faith. His virtual world will come crashing down under only one circumstance: revolution. At that point alone does it become evident just how far removed from reality a dictator – and his dictatorship – has been. A revolution is the moment of truth for a dictator, the moment when Gaddafi raged at the revolutionaries, "I am the person who has made Libya what it is today. Who are you?"[72] It was the moment when Mubarak said, "Me or chaos!"[73] and when Zine El Abidine Ben Ali (1936–2019), the former dictator of Tunisia, told the revolutionaries, "Now I understand you",[74] only to rush away with his family to his private jet and flee the country. It was the moment when a military tribunal read out to Ceaușescu a list of the massacres of thousands of innocent Romanians he had carried out. He barked back with his usual gruffness, "I do not recognise the trial. I will only speak to the Party Central Committee." And when they marched him out with his wife, Elena, for their execution, he screamed, "Have you forgotten what I have done for Romania? How can you treat your father like this?"[75]

Downfall

No matter how much chaos a revolution might bring with it, it is still the best way to end a dictatorship because it destroys the old regime completely in order to rebuild everything. However, revolutions rarely happen in history. Excepting those who die when in power, the usual end for a dictator is that he remains in supreme isolation in his virtual world until he makes a bad decision – one that eventually leads to a disaster and weakens his grip on the country.

During the Second World War, Mussolini's fateful decision was to invade Greece simply to prove that his armed forces were as strong as those of Hitler, and Hitler's was to attack the Soviet Union despite a clear warning from German intelligence officials about the consequences of such an attack. Saddam Hussein's error was to occupy Kuwait, and Bokassa's was opening fire on schoolchildren who were demonstrating about the extortionate cost of school uniforms (which they had to buy from a company owned by Bokassa's wife).[76] Gaddafi's mistake was to support terrorist organisations, which subjected Libya to years of economic sanctions and cost the country billions of dollars in compensation to its victims.

A dictator in his virtual and multi-delusional world is like a person driving a car with no brakes or rear-view mirror. He drives without the least notion of the surroundings he is driving through, and he cannot stop the car even if he wants to. Under these circumstances, the car will end up crashing horribly. Even if it does not happen today, then it will tomorrow or the next day.

The course of the dictatorship syndrome always starts off with a population that appears to need a dictator or is willing to accept him. The dictator then manages to achieve power and to place it all in his own hands. He passes through the stages of glory and supreme isolation and – except in the rare case of revolution – he inevitably ends up making a bad decision that leads to a catastrophe and for which everyone has to pay the price.

9

Prevention of the dictatorship syndrome

The relationship between a dictator and the masses, as with all human relationships, can be neither totally understood nor predicted. How does a dictator succeed in sweeping the masses along with him, in so completely dazzling their minds and their will that all he has to do is give a command and it is obeyed without a moment's hesitation? What is the nature of that feeling that drives millions of people into a state of somnambulant docility in which they carry out the will of one person? For all the explanations proffered by historians and social scientists, there is still something indefinable and difficult to predict here; human behaviour is shaped by life experience and not solely by theory.

That notwithstanding, the dictatorship syndrome – like many other illnesses – is preventable. To prevent dictatorship, we must be aware that – no matter how successful a dictator has been at the start – the end result will be catastrophic. We should reject a dictatorship as a matter of principle, without needing to wait for its results. Such an awareness will strip the dictator of the tools he uses to govern the masses – charisma, idols, religion, chauvinism and conspiracies – as outlined in this chapter.

Charisma

A dictator enjoys the sort of charisma that makes him appear miraculous and unique in the citizens' eyes. He is the brave and pugnacious hero, both the son of the people and their protecting father, who is cruel to be kind. He may seem to use his power sparingly even though the people have handed it over to him in order to save the country. He has a superhuman ability to work and to hold things together, and he seems to exhaust himself trying to make his people happy. He always knows things that the people do not, and he always seems to make the right decisions because the only things equal to his wisdom are his bravery and his devotion.

This gleaming, supernatural image of a dictator is sculpted and firmly anchored in the people's minds by the enormous propaganda machine, by means of thousands of articles in praise of him and thousands of images and recordings of him, all carefully shaped and crafted by the state intelligence agency so that the people can see their great leader in all types of attractive situations: orating to the millions, sitting down to eat with the poor, meeting the military leadership and the cabinet. His face portrays those important signs of gravity and decisiveness as he leans over to speak affectionately and caringly to a poor old woman or embraces a little girl who has just presented him with a bouquet, giving her a hug or patting her on the head in the loving attitude of a proud father.

Total control of the media is the *sine qua non* for the dictator's survival in power because, in addition to complete control over what information reaches the public, the media also brainwashes the people on a daily basis into thinking what the dictator wants them to think. For the dictator, the most important job of the media is to create and then polish that magical halo around the great leader. The masses cannot be led by a great leader if he is just an ordinary man prone to making mistakes. They will only yield to a hero of legendary proportions. It then follows that any criticism or objective analysis of a dictator's behaviour – even jokes and television satire – are all active ways of stripping away the magical image that he uses to control the masses. We know full well that the ruler is not some legendary hero but a normal person like us (no matter how special his abilities appear), and we know the importance of confronting a ruler with his mistakes rather than standing there singing hymns of praise to him. This awareness, which strips away the superhuman veneer of the dictator, is one way that, in the long run, will save us from dictatorship.

Idols

A dictator finds refuge in creating a pantheon of idols to which he accords absolute sanctity. He terms them the institutions of state, but they are in fact the long arms of the regime that he uses to wield power, and they generally consist of the army, police and judiciary. A dictator's media network never stops repeating stories of deeds of heroism (both true and false) carried out by the army and police, and broadcasts items extolling the integrity of the great judiciary for the whole world to see. The constant praise of these institutions in the dictator's media turns them into idols and places them legally and morally above any criticism or accountability.

Thereafter, if the topic of human rights violations by soldiers should be mentioned, the average brainwashed citizen will refuse to hold the soldiers accountable for having tortured innocent people or for having carried out extrajudicial killings. They will just trot out whatever line the media has fed them, "Even if the reports of torture are true, it must have been carried out by rogue individuals and the matter should be dealt with quietly and in a manner that does not affect the morale of our heroic troops who risk their lives for the country."[1] Dictatorships, naturally, do not allow for independent civil society.

The same is true when it comes to the temple of the judiciary. The average propaganda-sated individual will generally not bat an eyelid if a judge is accused of corruption, and they will repeat whatever expression they have heard from the media: "The enemies of the state want to undermine faith in our great judiciary with the aim of plunging our country into chaos." We need to remember, however, that the greatness of the judiciary must be more than an expression of its size. The judiciary is great when it fulfils the criterion of acting independently of the will of the governing body – whether democratic or not. If the judiciary is not independent, it has failed from a legal and ethical point of view.

The same holds for those in the police and army, whose service to the country is no greater than that of other professionals such as doctors, engineers, accountants – even barbers or street sweepers. Every last person deserves the same respect as a soldier as they are all honest workers doing their duty in the service of the state. Statements of praise should not cancel out accountability and, great as an army may be, this greatness should not prevent any single soldier being properly investigated should they make an error or commit a crime. If these notions were widely held among the people, a dictator's pantheon could not be created and his arsenal would be short of one weapon.

Religion

Some months after the Egyptians were defeated in 1967, students and workers rose up and held mass demonstrations for democracy. The defeat had plunged the broad swathe of the Egyptian population into a deep depression, a painful state of loss, frustration and incredulity.[2] They had believed in the project of their great leader, Nasser, for many years, and it had crumbled in front of their eyes like a sandcastle: the Egyptian army, which Nasser had convinced them had the greatest strike power in the Middle East, was destroyed within a few hours.

In the midst of this continued state of grief and hopelessness, on 2 April 1968, it was announced that the Virgin Mary had appeared above a church in the Zeitoun district.[3] This apparition was speedily confirmed by the church and, notably, the official media – completely under the control of the regime – also rushed to confirm the apparition, devoting to this miraculous event acres of newsprint and hours of radio and television time.[4] The phenomenon was discussed throughout Egypt and the church in question was thronged by thousands of Copts and Muslims (who also venerate the Virgin Mary). Stories were told of miracles happening every night, with people turning up at the church in their wheel-chairs and finding that, when they saw the apparition, they could stand up. There were reports of blind people's sight being restored as well as various other forms of illness being cured the moment the Virgin appeared.[5]

Fifty years after this event, it is difficult to discern the shape of the apparition in photographs taken at the time; the spots of light could easily have come from a projector somewhere nearby. Priests and the clergy might believe in the apparition of the Virgin by dint of their predisposition to a belief in miracles – but it is a different matter alto-gether for the secular Nasserite regime to wholeheartedly promote the story of the miracle of the apparition, particu-larly when some people believe that the whole business was set up and carried out by the intelligence agencies with the aim of diverting the nation's attention away from the previ-ous year's defeat and raising their morale.[6]

This episode underscores how the power of religion is used to thwart the critical thinking of the faithful. Those who, to this day, believe that the Virgin Mary appeared are intelligent and educated people, by they are seemingly inca-pable of thinking beyond their religious fallback positions, even in the face of a hundred pieces of incontrovertible evidence. They believe that the Virgin appeared because, in their heart of hearts, they want her to have appeared, and they will not allow any cracks to appear in their faith because they have built their lives, modelled their behav-iour and brought up their children on the precepts of that faith. When we defend our religious beliefs to a fault, we give up on the practice of logical thinking, meaning that if we perceive the smallest slight to the bedrock of our belief we may easily turn into fundamentalists, ever-ready to deny truths, defend patent nonsense, wage endless violent disputes and not only behave in a hostile manner but even let loose a flurry of outrageous diatribes on those who might question our religion.

Some Muslim jurisprudents have stated that the women's veil in its present form is not an Islamic obligation but the invention of Wahhabi shaykhs.[7] The evidence cited is that the veil was relatively uncommon in Egypt from the 1920s, but that that changed in the late 1970s when oil money started flowing into the country with the aim of promoting the Wahhabi school of thinking.[8] I once wrote as much on my Twitter feed and was subjected to hundreds of scathing comments from people accusing me of unbelief, licentiousness and of being an agent of World Zionism. Most of those who posted comments did not wish to debate what I had written, but were simply determined to direct a flood of insults against me with some of them even telephoning my office and pouring their vitriol down the line to my secretary to make sure that it actually reached me. This excessively hostile behaviour stems from fear. Fundamentalists behave in this way because they are genuinely afraid of losing their faith and live in mortal fear of being convinced of anything that might bruise their beliefs. Consequently a dictator in a Muslim-majority country has no better or more dangerous a weapon than religion. A dictator's weaponising of religion accords him even greater authority and makes it difficult, if not impossible, for people to take a stand against him or remove him from power because, in his use of religion, he has turned himself into God's representative and thus anyone against him is automatically against God.[9]

In the West, people fought a long battle to separate church and state, but such separation does not always exist in the Muslim world. Add to that the emergence of the Muslim Brothers in Egypt in 1928 and their adoption of political Islam (which has benefitted from the inflow of oil money since the 1970s) in order to convince millions of Egyptians of the notion of an Islamic caliphate and the necessity of fighting a *jihad* in order to establish it. This raises the prospect of a permanent state of war with non-Muslim states, but in the end the caliphate would, so they believe, raise the fluttering banner of Islam over the whole world. The notion of a caliphate is both a historical and a religious fiction as we have established earlier in this book, but nonetheless it is a dangerous notion that not only permits but encourages the use of violence against non-Muslims and promotes or enables religious dictators. Wahhabism does not recognise democracy but imposes on Muslims the duty of obedience to a Muslim ruler and forbids them to rise up against him, even should he be unjust and corrupt. Wahhabism provides the theoretical underpinning of terrorism. It provides all manner of justifications and rationales for religious authoritarianism and violence.[10]

As such, a dictator finds in religion the most lethal weapon he can use to concentrate his power until an undetermined time because religion, in addition to stifling believers' critical thinking, encourages them to live with injustice, teaching them to look instead to the perfect justice that exists only in the hereafter. The separation of religion and state is thus an essential condition for the prevention of dictatorship.

Chauvinism

Nicolas Chauvin was a French soldier in the army of Napoleon Bonaparte, and he became known for his desperate defence of all of Napoleon's decisions, even if they were contradictory. Even though some historians doubt the existence of any such person, the name Nicholas Chauvin became a byword for blind devotion and has given us the term chauvinism, meaning "the strong and unreasonable belief that your own country, sex or group is the best or most important".[11]

Patriotism is a natural, human feeling, but a dictator will always try to convert patriotism into chauvinism. His speeches will always assert that his nation is the greatest on earth and that it has a message to deliver to all humanity. Chauvinism titillates the masses who have a natural inclination towards self-praise and towards making a local strongman into a leader of historic dimensions. The most dangerous element of chauvinism is that it throws open the field to racism, terrorism, expansionist wars and a whole host of other crimes that can be committed in the name of a people, of a revolution, of a state or of a religion. If you have come to believe that you belong to an intellectual, ethnic or religious group that is superior to others, it might seem natural for you to deny others the rights you enjoy, as they are – to put it simply – inferior. By this logic, you might quite easily look the other way as they suffer discrimination or persecution.

The way to overcome chauvinism is to realise that there may well be a person who is superior to some others in one way or another, but there is no nation or people superior to any other as the criteria applied when judging individuals cannot be extrapolated to whole nations or on racial lines. As different as we all are in terms of our ethnicity, religion or thought systems, we are in the final analysis all human beings and equal in our rights and obligations. Standing up to chauvinism in any society will protect us from dictatorships.

Conspiracies

Conspiracy theories are the other face of chauvinism. Every dictator without exception has turned to the conspiracy theory, both believing in it and promulgating it. A dictator starts off by convincing some members of the public that they are greater than any other nation. He then persuades them that some evil people out there are plotting to stop them becoming world leaders.

As we have seen, a conspiracy theory demands the creation of such enemies – internal and/or external – and any dictator can resort to that in order to muster the masses behind him. He will then dehumanise his enemies rather than view them as individuals with an individual will and an independent character. They will always be portrayed as hostile groups of evildoers such as are found under any authoritarian regime with the proviso that, if the dictator is an Islamist, the plotters will be a mixture of Crusaders, Jews and Masons; if the dictator is a socialist, the plotters will be a mixture of capitalists and reactionaries. In the case of Hitler, the greatest conspiracy against the German *Volk* was that they were being exploited by world Jewry.[12]

A conspiracy theory can provide a number of positives to

a dictator, first and foremost being the spread of fear among the people that makes them even more attached to him as the only person capable of saving them. Second, it tars all his opponents with the mark of treachery and of being in thrall to evil plotters – and should a dictator make a decision with devastating consequences for the administration of the state, he can always dump the responsibility on these conspirators. Questioning a conspiracy theory will therefore deprive a dictator of one of his weapons. However, just because we dismiss a conspiracy theory, this does not mean that we think of the world beyond our own country as a paradise of philanthropic nations. Once we rid our brains of this conspiracy theory nonsense, we must realise that the phrase 'international relations' is simply a euphemism for the struggle over national interests. There is no conspiracy as such against any people or religion, but nation states are still in dispute over what they see as their interests and in most cases do not restrict themselves to the use of fine words alone.

Having a sense of awareness that resists the lure of charisma or idolatry of a leader or faith – in other words, having a healthy scepticism – is the most significant method of preventing dictatorship, although that is of course easier said than done. There is much ground to cover until humankind inexorably enjoys a time when there are no more dictators. At that time the world will be a better place – more just and more humane.

Notes

1 The syndrome

1. Robert Stephens, *Nasser: A Political Biography* (New York: Simon and Schuster, 1971), ch. 12.
2. Ibid. pp. 161, 295, 331, 342.
3. Ibid. pp. 492, 562.
4. Tensions between Syria and Nasser's regime existed from 1961 until 1966. In response to Israel's threat to Syria, Egypt and Syria formed the Joint Defence Agreement in 1966 with the support of the Soviet Union. See, in Arabic: Yusuf Muhammad and Fahd Abbas, *al-ʿIlāqāt al-sūriyya–al-miṣriyya* [Syrian–Egyptian Relations] <www.iasj. net/iasj?func=fulltext&aId=43677> and, in English, Michael Wall, 'Hussein and Nasser sign defence agreement – archive, 1967', *The Guardian*, 31 May 2019 <https://www.theguardian.com/world/2019/may/31/hussein-and-nasser-sign-defence-agreement-archive-1967>.
5. The following may be considered among Nasser's achievements: expansion of education and welfare services; encouragement of the spread of trade unions and cooperatives, although they remained under government control; and a government-backed industrialisation programme that included an iron and steel plant and hydroelectric power generated by the Aswan High Dam. See: Stephens, *Nasser*, pp. 187–88, 335, 364, 506, 559.
6. See: Stephens, *Nasser*, ch. 18.
7. Étienne de La Boetie, *The Politics of Obedience: The Discourse of Voluntary Servitude*, trans. Harry Kurz (New York: Free Life Editions, 1975).

8. Tawfīq al-Ḥakīm, *Shajrat al-ḥukm fī Miṣr 1919–1979* (Cairo: 1985). An English translation was published in 1985: Tawfiq al-Hakim, *The Return of Consciousness* (New York: New York University Press, 1985).

9. Ibid.

10. See, for example: Timothy Snyder, *On Tyranny: Twenty Lessons from the Twentieth Century* (London: Bodley Head, 2017) and 'How Dictators Keep Control', Seeker, 21 December 2011 <www.seeker.com/how-dictators-keep-control-discovery-news-1765571212.html>.

11. ʾAzzām Muḥammad Amīn, *al-Taḥlīl al-nafsī li-shakhṣiyyat al-ṭāghiyya al-mustabidd* [Psychological Analysis of the Personality of the Despot] <http://arabpsynet.com/Documents/DocAzzamPsychoanalysistTyrant.pdf>.

12. 'Freedom in the World 2017. Populists and Autocrats: The Dual Threat to Global Democracy', Freedom House <https://freedomhouse.org/report/freedom-world/freedom-world-2017>.

2 Symptoms of the dictatorship syndrome

1. See: Cynthia Johnston, 'Egypt orders cull of pigs over swine flu scare', Reuters, 29 April 2009 <https://www.reuters.com/article/ozatp-flu-egypt-idAFJOE53S0F520090429>.

2. Following Mubarak's decision to kill the pigs, a provincial governor ordered that a trench be dug and the pigs dumped into a caustic mixture. See: 'Egypt pigs meet cruel fate in swine flu cull', BBC News, 29 February 2009 <http://news.bbc.co.uk/1/hi/world/middle_east/8072953.stm>.

3. Ibid.

4. It was while visiting Menoufia University in November 2006 that Mubarak was introduced by the university Chancellor and then announced that he would amend the constitution. The university Chancellor, having earlier spoken against it, followed by supporting that decision. See, in Arabic: 'Mubārak yataʿahhid bi taʿdīl māda dastūriyya tanẓim intikhābāt al-riʾasa' [Mubarak Vows to Amend Constitutional Provision to Organize Presidential Elections], *Al Jazeera*, 19 November 2006 <https://bit.ly/2S2CSjX>.

5. An interview with ʻAlāʼ Farag Mugāhid can be found here: Daily Motion, *Miṣr fī usbūʼ: Ālāʼ Faraj... ayna hiya al-yawm?* [video], retrieved at <https://www.dailymotion.com/video/xr7e6e>. The story was also covered widely in the Arabic press. See, for example: Wajdy al-Kumi, ʻal-Ṭifla al-latī atlaqat ghaḍabhā ḍid Mubārak fī mawḍūʼ taʻbīr an 2016' [The Girl Who Expressed Her Anger Against Mubarak in an Essay on 2016], al-Youm al-Sabiʻ, 21 April 2011; ʻṬaliba miṣriyya tarsub fī imtiḥān bi sabab muhājamāt Amrīkā' [Egyptian Girl is Failed in her Examination for Attacking America], *Dunyā al-Waṭan*, 24 June 2006 <https://www.alwatanvoice.com/arabic/content/print/48782.html>.

6. Shirine al-Daydamouni, ʻArab women take to the "death boats" of illegal migration', *The Arab Weekly*, 2 December 2018 <https://thearabweekly.com/arab-women-take-death-boats-illegal-migration>.

3 The emergence of the good citizen

1. Adel Darwish and Gregory Alexander, *Unholy Babylon* (London: St. Martin's, 1991), p. 211.

2. This dialogue is recounted in Ahmed Mansour's interview with one of Saddam's ministers, Salah Omar al-Ali, *Witness to an Era* [video], broadcast in nine parts on *Al Jazeera Arabic*:
   Part 1: <https://youtu.be/iyeDZiC481E>
   Part 2: <https://youtu.be/OTd6uejM0Fg>
   Part 3: <https://youtu.be/DoE9_HB9VnU>
   Part 4: <https://youtu.be/02XUBsMVrCI>
   Part 5: <https://youtu.be/rngkqpJ0Dhw>
   Part 6: <https://youtu.be/ZSZW5XUek5k>
   Part 7: <https://youtu.be/gBAQ6V8t_c4>
   Part 8: <https://youtu.be/8jBGxizY7w8>
   Part 9: <https://youtu.be/rwzVxXfCvRc>

3. See: Giles Milton, *Fascinating Footnotes from History* (London: John Murray, 2015).

4. See: Peter Theo Curtis, ʻPeter Theo Curtis's Writing on The Twisted, Terrifying Last Days of Assad's Syria', *The New*

Republic, 4 October 2011 <https://newrepublic.com/article/95722/ syria-damascus-bashar-basil-al-assad-sunni-alawi>.

5. See: Randall Fegley, 'The U.N. Human Rights Commission: The Equatorial Guinea Case', *Human Rights Quarterly*, vol. 3, no. 1 (1981), p. 37.

6. This account is from an unpublished memoir by one of the revolutionaries, for which I was asked to write an introduction. I keep the author's name anonymous here for reasons that require no further explanation.

7. Mario de Queiroz, 'PORTUGAL: Salazar "Greatest Portuguese Ever", TV Viewers Say', *Inter Press Service (IPS)*, 30 March 2007 <http://www.ipsnews.net/2007/03/portugal-salazar-greatest-portuguese-ever-tv-viewers-say/>.

8. Ibid. See also: Peter Walker, 'The "great" dictator', *The Guardian*, 26 March 2007 <https://www.theguardian.com/news/blog/2007/mar/26/ salazar>.

9. The name of the song is 'Papa Bokassa Notre Père'. It is discussed, in French, here: France Inter, *Hymne à Bokassa 1er – Un Temps de Pauchon* [video], retrieved at <www.youtube.com/ watch?v=VoGJugoAHKM>.

4 The conspiracy theory

1. 'The Protocols of the Learned Elders of Zion', *Wikisource* <https:// en.wikisource.org/wiki/The_Protocols_of_the_Learned_Elders_of_ Zion#Protocol_I_The_Basic_Doctrine>, accessed 24 September 2019.

2. See: 'Protocols of the Elders of Zion', Holocaust Encyclopedia, United States Holocaust Memorial Museum <https:// encyclopedia.ushmm.org/content/en/article/protocols-of-the-elders-of-zion>; Brigitte Sion, 'Protocols of Elders of Zion', My Jewish Learning <www.myjewishlearning.com/article/ protocols-of-the-elders-of-zion>.

3. Leon Poliakov, 'Elders of Zion, Protocols of the Learned', *Encyclopaedia Judaica*, 2nd ed., vol. 6, p. 297.

4. 'A speech at the Siemens Dynamo Works in Berlin, 10 November 1933', BBC History <http://www.bbc.co.uk/history/worldwars/genocide/hitler_audio.shtml>.

5. Audio provided by Alerta Judiada, 'Adolf Hitler Fought the Bank', *Internet Archive*. Translation from 'I Am Anti-zionist' <https://similarworlds.com/8946996-I-Am-Anti-zionist/974929-Yes-Germany-was-back-then-a-democracy-before-us>.

6. A case in point would be the well-known Egyptian television miniseries *Horseman Without A Horse*, which centres on *The Protocols of the Learned Elders of Zion*. The series was first broadcast in 2002 and subsequently rebroadcast. See: 'Egyptian Television Re-Airs Anti-Semitic Miniseries "Horseman Without A Horse"', 5 April 2012 <www.adl.org/blog/egyptian-television-re-airs-anti-semitic-miniseries-horseman-without-a-horse>.

7. Two examples (in Arabic) include: *Jarā'im al-yahūd wa ifsādhum fī majāl al-nafs* [The Crimes of Jews and Their Corruption of Psychology], IslamWeb, 15 April 2002 <http://articles.islamweb.net/media/index.php?page=article&lang=A&id=14037>; *Jarā'im al-Yahūd wa ghadrhum* [The Crimes and Treachery of the Jews], Midād, 8 November 2007 <https://bit.ly/2UpObVr>.

8. "[Ceauşescu] didn't believe they were doing this on their own … the Americans and Russians got together to do this." See: Soraya Sarhaddi Nelson, '25 Years After Death, A Dictator Still Casts A Shadow In Romania', National Public Radio, 24 December 2014 <www.npr.org/sections/parallels/2014/12/24/369593135/25-years-after-death-a-dictator-still-casts-ashadow-in-romania>.

9. This speech can be viewed here: *Muammar Gaddafi addresses the nation* [video], 27 January 2014, retrieved at <www.youtube.com/watch?v=cnQ1bErKvsQ>.

10. Regime supporters are seen to confront perceived adversaries at the journalists' syndicate: *Citizens surround the Journalists' Syndicate* [video], 4 May 2016, retrieved at <https://youtu.be/T4AuiMwd7J8>; *Citizens outside the Journalists' Syndicate taunt el-Sisi* [video], Al Tahrir, 4 May 2016, retrieved at <https://youtu.be/DLGmnj3b21I>. See also: *Citizens surround the entrance of the Journalists' Syndicate*

[video], al-Youm al-sabi', 4 May 2016, retrieved at <https://bit. ly/2FrUd4d>.

11. Examples can be seen in the BBC documentary *Vladimir Putin: The World's Most Powerful President* [video], 12 September 2016, retrieved at <https://youtu.be/NOCJENwsdJw>.

12. This slogan was voiced in a statement by Nasser to the nation on 30 March 1968. See: 'Gamal Abdel Nasser's statement to the Nation' <http://nasser.bibalex.org/Data/GR09_1/Speeches/1968/680330_ bayanat.htm>.

13. Claudia Koonz, *The Nazi Conscience* (Cambridge, London: Harvard University Press, 2003), p. 20.

14. See: David Jones, 'Why the hell should I feel sorry, says girl soldier who abused Iraqi prisoners at Abu Ghraib prison', *The Daily Mail*, 13 June 2009 <www.dailymail.co.uk/news/article-1192701/ Why-hell-I-feel-sorry-says-girl-soldier-abused-Iraqi-prisoners-Abu-Ghraib-prison.html>.

15. Gustav Niebuhr, 'HIROSHIMA; Enola Gay's Crew Recalls The Flight Into a New Era', *The New York Times*, 6 August 1995 <https:// www.nytimes.com/1995/08/06/world/hiroshima-enola-gay-s-crew-recalls-the-flight-into-a-new-era.html?pagewanted=all>.

16. See, in Arabic: 'Ukāsha: al-ikhwān 'umalā' Amrīkā fī Miṣr [Ukāsha: The Brotherhood Are America's Agents in Egypt], *Dunya al-waṭan*, 31 March 2012 <www.alwatanvoice.com/arabic/content/ print/265320.html>; Su'āl amrīkānī: hal Trump 'amīl mithl al-Sīsī [An American Question: Is Trump an Agent, Like Sisi?], Freedom and Justice Gate, 17 July 2018 <https://bit.ly/2UqJ4Eg>.

17. See: Muḥammad Abū al-Ghayṭ, bi'l-fidiyū wa'l-ṣuwar: al-shafarat al-sirriyya min "al-ḥaẓāẓa al-māsūniyya" wa ḥattā "ḥalawānī ikhwān [In Photos and Videos: Secret Codes from the Masonic Hoards and Even the Halawani Brothers], *Shorouk*, 21 January 2014 <www. shorouknews.com/news/view.aspx?cdate=20012014&id=87273ac4-f055-4150-851fb2221b20dd39>.

18. Ibid.

5 The spread of the fascist mindset

1. Dr Muḥammad al-Bāz, *Ṣaḥāfat al-ithāra: al-Siyāsa wa al-Dīn wa al-Jins fī al-Ṣuḥuf al-Miṣriyya* [The Sensationalist Press: Politics, Religion and Sex in the Egyptian Press] (Cairo, 2012).

2. Robert Stephens, *Nasser: A Political Biography* (New York: Simon and Schuster, 1971), pp. 88, 127, 155, 295, 299, 397, 415, 533.

3. ʿAbd al-Nāṣir yaṣdur qarār taʾmīm al-ṣaḥāfa [Nasser issues a decree nationalising the press], trans. Russell Harris, 24 May 2016 <https://www.vetogate.com/2201209>.

4. Lamʿi al-Muṭīʿī, *Mawsūʿat Nisāʾ wa rijāl min Miṣr* [Encyclopaedia of Women and Men from Egypt] (Cairo: Dar al-Shorouk, 1968), p. 215.

5. See: Maḥmūd al-Qayʿī, Najl al-kātib al-kabīr Iḥsān ʿAbd al-Quddūs li "Raʾy al-Yawm": ʿAbd al-Nāṣir ittaṣṣal hātifiyyan bi Abī baʿd khurūjihi min al-muʿtaqal wa qāl lahu: Itʿadabt yā Iḥsān? [The Son of the Great Writer Ihsan Abd al-Quddous to *Raʾy al-youm*: Abd al-Nasser Telephoned My Father After His Release from Prison and Said to Him: Did You Learn Your Lesson, Ihsan?] *Raʾy al-youm*, 28 January 2018 <https://bit.ly/2A3Ahi2>. In addition to what his son details, Ihsan also personally informed my father in confidence that he had been tortured.

6. Ami Ayalon, *The Press in the Arab Middle East: A History* (New York and Oxford: Oxford University Press, 1995), p. 245.

7. See: *Sisi attacks the Egyptian media* [video], Al Jazeera, 1 November 2015, retrieved at <www.youtube.com/watch?v=tFejXv_QgfQ>.

8. Joseph Goebbels, 'Der Vollzug des Volkswillens', trans. Barbara Schwepcke, *Völkischer Beobachter*, 12 May 1933.

9. Encyclopedia.com defines the 'Soviet man', or 'builder of communism', as 'educated, hardworking, collectivistic, patriotic, and unfailingly loyal to the Communist Party of the Soviet Union'. See 'soviet man', Encyclopedia.com <https://www.encyclopedia.com/history/encyclopedias-almanacs-transcripts-and-maps/soviet-man>, accessed 25 September 2019.

10. A. Robert Rogers, 'Censorship and Libraries in the Soviet Union', *Journal of Library History, Philosophy, and Comparative Librarianship*, vol. 8, no. 1 (1973), p. 24.

11. See: Denis Mack Smith, *Mussolini* (London: Paladin, 1983), p. 91.
12. Details of the revisions can be found, in Arabic, here: al-Maḥkama al-ʿUlyā al-Miṣriyya [Case No. 7 of the Supreme Court, Judicial Year 2: "Constitutional"], University of Minnesota, Human Rights Library <http://hrlibrary.umn.edu/arabic/Egypt-SCC-SC/Egypt-SC2-Y7.html>.
13. The constitutional debate is discussed, in Arabic, here: Yaḥya al-Jammāl, Ḥurriyat al-iʿtiqād [The Freedom of Belief], *al-Ahram*, 6 November 2014 <www.ahram.org.eg/NewsQ/336294.aspx>.
14. Zakī Abū Shādī, 'Li mā dhā anā muʾmin' (Alexandria: Maktabat al-taʿāwun, 1937).
15. Muḥammad Farīd Wajdī, 'Li mā dhā anā muʾmin', 1937.
16. See: 'Egypt: Unprecedented crackdown on freedom of expression under al-Sisi turns Egypt into open-air prison', Amnesty International, 20 September 2018 <https://www.amnesty.org/en/latest/news/2018/09/egypt-unprecedented-crackdown-on-freedom-of-expression-under-alsisi-turns-egypt-into-openair-prison/>.
17. See: 'Egypt: An open-air prison for critics', *Amnesty International Public Statement*, Amnesty International, 20 September 2018, p. 1.
18. See: Ghada Tantawi and Mariam Rizk, 'Egypt takes harsh line towards artists and authors', BBC News, 20 April 2016 <https://www.bbc.co.uk/news/world-middle-east-36039529>.
19. See: 'Cairo book protesters released', BBC News, 12 May 2000 <http://news.bbc.co.uk/1/hi/world/middle_east/746766.stm>, and, in Arabic: Māhir Ḥasan, Walīma li aʿshāb al-baḥr [A Banquet for Seaweed – a novel against everyone], *al-Masry al-youm*, 26 June 2017 <www.almasryalyoum.com/news/details/1154353>.
20. See, in Arabic: 'Al-Azhar condemns Ḥaydar's Banquet', *Al-Bayān*, 18 May 2000 <https://www.albayan.ae/last-page/2000–05–18–1.1068046>.

6 The dislocation of the intellectual

1. This widely repeated phrase is a misquotation from Hanns Johst's pro-Nazi play *Schlageter* (1933).

2. The editors, 'From the Stacks: "Homage to Thomas Mann"', *The New Republic*, 12 August 2013 <https://newrepublic.com/article/114269/thomas-mann-stands-anti-semitism-stacks>.

3. See: Pete Ayrton, ed. *No Man's Land: Fiction from a World at War* (London: Serpent's Tail, 2014).

4. See: Sheila Fitzpatrick, 'Like a Thunderbolt', Review of *Aleksandr Solzhenitsyn* by Liudmila Saraskina, *London Review of Books*, vol. 30, no. 17 (2008), pp. 13–15.

5. See: 'Aleksandr Isayevich Solzhenitsyn', *Britannica* <https://www.britannica.com/biography/Aleksandr-Solzhenitsyn>, accessed 2 October 2019.

6. See: Ashifa Kassam, 'Federico García Lorca was killed on official orders, say 1960s police files', *The Guardian*, 23 April 2015 <www.theguardian.com/culture/2015/apr/23/federico-garcia-lorca-spanish-poet-killed-orders-spanish-civil-war>.

7. Antonio Gramsci, 'General Introduction', in Quintin Hoare and Geoffrey Nowell Smith, eds. and trans. *Selections from the Prison Notebooks* (New York: International Publishers, 1971).

8. Ibid.

9. Adam Feinstein, *Pablo Neruda: A Passion for Life* (New York: Bloomsbury, 2004), p. 353.

10. Blackshirts were militant squads of Italian fascists that brought Benito Mussolini to power. See 'blackshirt' in *Britannica* <www.britannica.com/topic/Blackshirt>, accessed 23 October 2019.

11. See: Luigi Barzini, 'How Pirandello Became Pirandellian (And Other Things)', *The New York Times*, 25 March 1973 <https://www.nytimes.com/1973/03/25/archives/how-pirandello-became-pirandellian-and-other-things-barzini-on.html>.

12. See: Stéphanie Panichelli-Batalla, 'When Gabriel García Márquez met Fidel Castro', *The Independent*, 14 December 2016 <https://www.independent.co.uk/arts-entertainment/books/features/fidel-castro-gabrielgarcia-marquez-a7474596.html>.

13. "Fidel is the sweetest man I know," quoted in Emily Temple, 'On Fidel Castro's Friendships with Literary Giants', *Literary Hub*,

28 November 2016 <https://lithub.com/on-fidel-castros-friendships-with-literary-giants>.

14. Panichelli-Batalla, 'When Gabriel Garcîa Márquez met Fidel Castro'.

15. Martin Vennard, 'How the CIA secretly published Dr Zhivago', BBC World Service, 24 June 2014 <https://www.bbc.co.uk/news/magazine-27942646>.

16. Erin Blakemore, 'Why Boris Pasternak Rejected His Nobel Prize', JSTOR Daily, 18 February 2015 <https://daily.jstor.org/why-boris-pasternak-rejected-his-nobel-prize/>.

17. Ben Panko, 'How Boris Pasternak Won and Lost the Nobel Prize', Smithsonian, 23 October 2017 <https://www.smithsonianmag.com/smart-news/how-boris-pasternak-won-and-lost-nobel-prize-180965368/#2Jqk9kRf3fM4Kp>.

18. See, in Arabic: Rajā' al-Naqqāsh, *Ṣafḥāt min mudhakkirāt Najīb Maḥfūẓ* [Pages from the Memoirs of Naguib Mahfouz] (Cairo: Dār al-Shorouk, 2011).

19. Samia Mehrez, 'Respected Sir', *Egyptian Writers between History and Fiction: Essays on Naguib Mahfouz, Sonallah Ibrahim, and Gamal al-Ghitani* (Cairo; New York: The American University in Cairo Press, 1994, 2005), p. 26.

20. 'Kitāb 'an Maḥfūẓ yakshif ra'yahu fī 'Abd al-Nāṣir alladhī rafaḍ muṣādarat a'mālahu' [Book about Mahfouz reveals his opinion of Abdel Nasser who refused to ban his books], Reuters, 25 December 2011 <https://ara.reuters.com/article/entertainmentNews/idARACAE7B005X20111225>.

21. Sayed Mahmoud, 'Egyptian former minister returns Gaddafi Int'l Award for Literature', Ahram Online, 26 February 2011 <http://english.ahram.org.eg/News/6474.aspx>.

22. See, in Arabic: Kāmil Kāmil, Ma'ārik al-islāmiyīn ma' wizārat al-thaqāfa [The Battles of the Islamists with the Ministry of Culture], *al-Youm al-sābi'*, 4 October 2015 <https://bit.ly/2rtBWK8>.

23. See, for example, a 2016 report by Human Rights Watch: '"We Are in Tombs": Abuses in Egypt's Scorpion Prison', Human Rights Watch, 28 September 2019 <https://www.hrw.org/report/2016/09/28/we-are-tombs/abuses-egypts-scorpion-prison>.

24. See: Chris Stephen, 'Muammar Gaddafi war crimes files revealed', *The Guardian*, 18 June 2011 <https://www.theguardian.com/world/2011/jun/18/muammar-gaddafi-war-crimes-files>.

25. See, in Arabic: Shaʿbān Yūsuf, 'Salmāwī wa ʿaṣfūr wa qindīl wa al-raḥbānī: muthaqqafūn fī balāṭ al-Qadhāfī' [Salmāwī, ʿAṣfūr, Qindīl and al-Raḥbāmī: Intellectuals in the Court of Gaddafi], *Ahl al-Qurʾān*, 27 August 2011 <www.ahl-alquran.com/arabic/show_news.php?main_id=19417>.

26. See, in French: Jérôme Garcin, 'Goytisolo, l'écrivain qui a dit non à Kadhafi', *Bibliobs*, 11 April 2011 <https://bibliobs.nouvelobs.com/la-tendance-de-jerome-garcin/20110406.0BS0861/goytisolo-1-ecrivain-qui-a-dit-non-a-kadhafi.html.>; and, in English: Boyd Tonkin, 'Boyd Tonkin: The writer who said no to Libyan loot', *The Independent*, 4 September 2009 <https://www.independent.co.uk/arts-entertainment/books/features/boyd-tonkin-the-writer-who-said-no-to-libyan-loot-1781192.html>.

27. See, in Arabic: 'ʿAṣfūr ithnāʾ tasallumihi jāʾizat al-Qadhāfī: fuztu bi 'l-jāʾiza thalāth marrāt' [Asfour When He Won the Gaddafi Prize: "I won the prize three times"] *Middle East Online*, 25 April 2010 <https://bit.ly/2Ut421V>.

28. Nassif al-Nasseri, 'Saddam, you are the one we have waited for', trans. Russell Harris, *Asfār*, April 1992.

29. Ṣalāḥ ʿĪsā, *Muthaqqafūn wa ʿaskar: murājaʿāt wa tajārib wa shahādāt ʿan ḥālat al-muthaqqafīn fī ẓill ḥukm ʿAbd al-Nāṣir* [Intellectuals and the Military] (Cairo, 1986), pp. 9–10.

7 Dictatorship and the predisposing factors for terrorism

1. Qur'an 2:216 trans. Abdullah Yusuf Ali.

2. See, for example: Adam Withnall, 'Isis video purports to show beheadings and execution at gunpoint of 30 Ethiopian Christians and destruction of churches in Libya', *The Independent*, 19 April 2005 <https://www.independent.co.uk/news/world/middle-east/isis-video-shows-beheadings-and-execution-at-gunpoint-of-30-ethiopian-christians-and-destruction-of-10187749.html> and Eyder

Paralta, 'Retaliating For Killings, Egypt Launches Airstrikes Against ISIS In Libya', *NPR*, 16 February 2015 <https://www.npr.org/sections/thetwo-way/2015/02/16/386669949/retaliating-for-killings-egypt-launches-air-strikes-against-isis-in-libya?t=1566998680386>.

3. Gustave Le Bon, *La civilisation des Arabes*, trans. Russell Harris (Paris: Librairie de Firmin-Didot et Cie, 1884), pp. 126–127.

4. Ibid.

5. Ibid.

6. The following news reports reference the word 'nice' in relation to the terror suspects in question: Fox News, 'Terror suspect's NJ mosque has been under NYPD surveillance: Report', 1 November 2017<https://www.foxnews.com/us/terror-suspects-nj-mosque-has-been-under-nypd-surveillance-report>; Julian Isherwood, 'Suspect was "a nice lad who would not be capable of hijacking"', *The Telegraph*, 2 September 2002 <www.telegraph.co.uk/news/worldnews/1406044/Suspect-was-a-nice-lad-who-would-not-becapable-of-hijacking.html>; Daniel Tedford, 'Colorado shooting suspect described as "smart" and "nice" honor student at UC Riverside', *Daily Breeze*, 20 July 2012 <https://www.dailybreeze.com/2012/07/20/colorado-shooting-suspect-described-as-smart-and-nice-honor-student-at-uc-riverside/>; Stephanie Balloo, 'Friends of Westminster terror suspect Salih Khater say he was "very nice man" and is innocent', *Birmingham Live*, 15 August 2018 <www.birminghammail.co.uk/news/midlands-news/friends-westminster-terror-suspect-salih-15031630>.

7. Robert Stephens, *Nasser: A Political Biography* (New York: Simon and Schuster, 1971), p. 341.

8. NasserSpeeches, *Kalimat al-ra'īs Jamāl 'Abd al-Nāṣir bi sha'n al-infiṣāl 'an Sūriyā* [video], [Gamal Abdel Nasser's statement on breaking with Syria], 7 January 2012, retrieved at <https://www.youtube.com/watch?v=U0wr0kCtZyQ>.

9. William H. Brackney, *Human Rights and the World's Major Religions* (California: Praeger, 2013), p. 201.

10. See, for example, the case of Marwa Ali El-Sherbini who was murdered in Germany. Kate Connolly and Jack Shenker, 'The headscarf martyr: murder in German court sparks Egyptian fury',

The Guardian, 7 July 2009 <www.theguardian.com/world/2009/jul/07/german-trial-hijab-murder-egypt>. See also the Organization for Security and Co-operation in Europe's report *Hate crime against Muslims*, 22 February 2018 <https://www.osce.org/odihr/373441?download=true>.

11. See: Office of the Coordinator for Counterterrorism, 'National Counterterrorism Center: Annex of Statistical Information', Country Reports on Terrorism 2011, 31 July 2012 <www.state.gov/j/ct/rls/crt/2011>; Ruth Alexander and Hannah Moore, 'Are most victims of terrorism Muslim?' BBC News, 20 January 2015 <www.bbc.com/news/magazine-30883058>; 'Muslims the highest victims of terrorism', *World Bulletin*, 19 November 2015 <https://www.worldbulletin.net/islamophobia/muslims-the-highest-victims-of-terrorism-h166494.html>.

12. See, in Arabic: 'Rasāʾil al-imām al-shahīd Ḥasan al-Bannā' [Epistles of the Martyred Iman Hasan al-Banna] <https://bit.ly/2TF4cWe>.

13. See: Hugh Kennedy, *The Prophet and the Age of the Caliphates: The Islamic Near East from the Sixth to the Eleventh Century* (Oxon and New York: Routledge, 2016), p. 127; John Alden Williams trans. *The History of al-Ṭabarī, Volume 27: The ʿAbbāsid Revolution, A.D. 743–750/A.H. 126–132* (New York: State University of New York Press, 1985).

14. Ibn al-Sāʿī, *Kitāb mukhtaṣar akhbār al-khulafāʾ* [An Abridged History of the Caliphs] (Bulaq, 1891), p. 10.

15. 'Madhābiḥ al-ʿUthmāniyīn fī Miṣr [Ottoman Massacres in Egypt] *al-Youm al-sābiʿ*, 2 November 2014 <https://bit.ly/2AU4jGI>.

16. This is attested to, for example, in *Kitāb al-aghānī* (*The Book of Songs*) by Abū al-Faraj al-Iṣfahānī (897–967), a multivolume collection of poems and songs. Several contemporary published editions include Dar al-Shaʿb and Dār Būlāq in Cairo and Dār al-Miṣriyya al-Lubnāniyya and Dār Ṣādir in Beirut. Please see also 'The Book of Songs', *World Digital Library* <https://www.wdl.org/en/item/7442/>, accessed 31 August 2019.

17. Ibid.

18. Zachary Laub, 'Egypt's Muslim Brotherhood', Council on Foreign Relations, 15 August 2019 <https://www.cfr.org/backgrounder/egypts-muslim-brotherhood>, accessed 1 October 2019.

19. Ohad Gozani, 'Bomber's mission "dedicated to Iraqi people"', *The Telegraph*, 31 March 2003 <https://www.telegraph.co.uk/news/worldnews/middleeast/israel/1426206/Bombers-mission-dedicated-to-Iraqi-people.html>.

20. See, for example: Helena Horton and Emily Allen, 'Everything we know about the Finsbury Park mosque terror attack', *The Telegraph*, 20 June 2017 <https://www.telegraph.co.uk/news/2017/06/19/everything-know-finsbury-park-mosque-terror-attack/>; 'Christchurch shootings: Mosque attacker charged with terrorism', BBC News, 21 May 2019 <https://www.bbc.co.uk/news/world-asia-48346786>; *Hate crime against Muslims*, OSCE ODIHR <www.osce.org/odihr/373441?download=true>.

21. See, for example, this blog post on a Salafi website (in Arabic): ʿAbd al-Raḥmān ibn ʿAbd al-Khāliq, 'al-Hujūm ʿalā al-Islām min man? wa li mā dhā?' [Who is attacking Islam? And why?] <www.salafi.net/articles/article15.html>.

22. See: Phyllis Bennis, 'February 15, 2003. The Day the World Said No to War', Institute for Policy Studies, 15 February 2013 <https://ips-dc.org/february_15_2003_the_day_the_world_said_no_to_war>; Abdalla F. Hassan, 'Police Outnumber Antiwar Protesters in Cairo', *World Press Review*, 30 January 2003 <www.worldpress.org/Mideast/922.cfm>.

23. Noam Chomsky, 'As long they get the backing of dictators, it doesn't matter to western governments what Arab populations think', *The Guardian*, 31 August 2011 <www.theguardian.com/commentisfree/video/2011/aug/31/noam-chomsky-terrorism-video>.

24. Ibid.

25. See: Ted Galen Carpenter, 'How Washington Funded the Taliban', Cato Institute, 2 August 2002 <https://www.cato.org/publications/commentary/how-washington-funded-taliban>.

26. See: 'Holocaust survivor Reuven Moskovitz joins flotilla to run Israel's blockade', *The Weekend Australian*, 28 September 2010 <https://www.theaustralian.com.au/news/world/

holocaust-survivor-reuven-moskovitz-joins-flotilla-to-run-
israels-blockade/news-story/99762d6bffa3a97354db84719
85f4994>.

27. See, in Arabic: Manāf Maḥmūd Qawmān, 'Istiqbāl Almāniyā
li'l-lāji ʿīn... dāfiʿ insānī um maṣlaḥa qawmiyya?' [Is Germany's
Acceptance of Refugees: Motivated by Humanitarianism or National
Interest?], 18 October 2015 <https://bit.ly/2CdrY4k>.

28. See, in Arabic: Aḥmad ʿUbayd, 'Ẓāhirat iʿtināq al-masīḥiyya bayn
al-lāji ʿīn... Īymān um manfaʿa?' [The Phenomenon of Refugees
Converting to Christianity: Faith or Self-Interest?], Syria.tv, 16
March 2016 <https://bit.ly/2ACfGCP>.

29. Khaled al-Barri, *al-Dunya Ajmal min al-Janna* (Cairo, 2006).
Available in English as: Khaled al-Berry, *Life Is More Beautiful than
Paradise: A Jihadist's Own Story*, trans. Humphrey Davies (London:
Haus Publishing, 2009).

30. Khaled al-Berry, *Life Is More Beautiful than Paradise*, p. 94.

31. Ibid, p. 98.

32. Ibid, p. 154.

33. For example, Ayman al-Zawahiri, the leader of al-Qaeda, was
tortured in Egypt as detailed in Montasser al-Zayyat's book *Ayman
al-Zawahiri as I Knew Him* (Cairo: Dār Miṣr al-Maḥrūsa, 2002).
It was translated from the Arabic by Ahmed Fekry under the title
The Road to al-Qaeda: The Story of Bin Laden's Right-Hand Man
(London: Pluto Press, 2004). There are other examples: Salih
Saraya, who led the Military Academy group (Tanzīm al-Fanniya
al-ʿAskariyya), believed that the defeat of Zionism depended on the
establishment of an Islamic state in Egypt. Other sources include:
Ahmed Ra'if, *The Black Gate (al-Bawāba al-sawdāʾ)* (Cairo:
al-Zahrāʾ li'l-Iʿlām al-ʿArabī, 1986); Gilles Kepel, *Muslim Extremism
in Egypt: The Prophet and Pharaoh*, trans. Jon Rothschild (Berkley
and Los Angeles: University of California Press, 2003).

8 The course of the syndrome

1. An instructive parallel may be found in the work of Algerian writer and philosopher Malek Bennabi (1905–1973) who explores why certain societies have been prone to colonisation. He outlines these ideas in *Les conditions de la renaissance* (1948). See also, as earlier discussed, Étienne de La Boétie's essay *The Discourse of Voluntary Servitude* (1576).

2. Ayatollah Ruhollah Khomeini lays out his vision for theocratic rule in his book *Governance of the Jurist: Islamic Government*, published in English by The Institute for Compilation and Publication of Imam Khomeinie's works (International Division), Tehran.

3. The following histories of the Gulf kingdoms make this argument: Karen Elliott House, *On Saudi Arabia: Its People, Past, Religion, Fault Lines – and Future* (New York: Alfred A. Knopf, 2012); Farah Al-Naqib, *Kuwait Transformed: A History of Oil and Urban Life* (Stanford: Stanford University Press, 2016); Allen J. Fromherz, *Qatar: A Modern History* (London: I.B.Tauris, 2017).

4. Al-Naqib, *Kuwait Transformed.*

5. Fromherz, *Qatar: A Modern History.*

6. GDP per capita in the Gulf states is among the highest in the world: Qatar, $124,500; United Arab Emirates, $67,700; Kuwait, $66,200; Saudi Arabia, $54,800; Bahrain, $48,500; Oman, $45,200. See: CIA World Factbook <https://www.cia.gov/library/publications/the-world-factbook/rankorder/2004rank.html>, accessed 1 September 2019.

7. In Saudi Arabia, for example, "an antiterrorism bill proposed in July 2011 included a minimum 10-year prison sentence for 'questioning the integrity' of the king or crown prince". See 'Saudi Arabia', *Freedom House* <https://freedomhouse.org/report/freedom-press/2013/saudi-arabia>; 'Saudi reporter jailed for five years for insulting rulers: Amnesty', *Reuters*, 27 March 2016 <www.reuters.com/article/us-saudicourt-idUSKCN0WT0AM>. Also, in 2012, Qatari poet Rashid al-Ajami was sentenced to life in prison for reciting a poem that was considered critical of the emir. See 'Qatari poet freed after three years in jail for reciting poem allegedly insulting emir', *The Guardian*, 26 March 2016 <https://www.

theguardian.com/world/2016/mar/17/qatari-poet-freed-after-three-years-in-jail-for-reciting-poem-allegedly-insulting-emir>.

8. See: David D. Kirkpatrick, *Into the Hands of the Soldiers: Freedom and Chaos in Egypt and the Middle East* (New York: Viking, 2018).

9. Ten Most Populous Countries in the Middle East, WorldAtlas <https://www.worldatlas.com/articles/ten-most-populous-countries-in-the-middle-east.html>.

10. See: Kirkpatrick, *Into the Hands of the Soldiers*.

11. See Lawrence Squeri, 'The Italian Local Elections of 1920 and the Outbreak of Fascism', *The Historian*, vol. 45, no. 3 (1983), pp. 324–336.

12. There are other interpretations of the phrase. See, for example: 'Pan o palo', *Britannica* <https://www.britannica.com/topic/pan-o-palo>, accessed 23 October 2019.

13. The origins of the French Revolution of 1789, for instance, were widespread famine and starvation in rural areas and bread riots in Paris. Similarly, bread riots broke out in Egypt in January 1977 following the end of basic food subsidies in a move mandated by the World Bank and the International Monetary Fund.

14. See, for example, reports by Dr Alice Miller, available at *The Natural Child Project* <https://www.naturalchild.org/articles/alice_miller/>.

15. Hoda Abdel Nasser, 'A Historical Sketch of Gamal Abdel Nasser', Site for President Gamal Abdel Nasser, in cooperation with Bibliotheca Alexandrina and the Gamal Abdel Nasser Foundation <http://nasser.bibalex.org/Common/pictures01-%20sira_en.htm#1>.

16. This remark can be heard, in Arabic, in this video: *al-Sisi meets the media in New York Today – special to Qanāt al-Taḥrīr* [video], 9 October 2014, retrieved at <www.youtube.com/watch?v=bokJs9Duwxo>.

17. Louis Sell, *Slobodan Milosevic and the Destruction of Yugoslavia* (Durham and London: Duke University Press, 2002), p. 16.

18. Quoted from 'Childhood Trauma' by Alice Miller. This article was presented as a lecture at the Lexington 92nd Street YWHA in New York City on 22 October 1998. See: <https://www.naturalchild.org/alice_miller/childhood_trauma.html>.

19. Margaret Litvin, *Hamlet's Arab Journey: Shakespeare's Prince and Nasser's Ghost* (Princeton: Princeton University Press, 2011) p. 39.

20. "Egypt, too, in the same manner, conceived and bore in her belly an awesome child. The Egypt that had slept for centuries in a single day arose to her feet. She had been waiting, as the Frenchman said, waiting for her beloved son, the symbol of her buried sorrows and hopes, to be born anew. And this beloved was born again from the body of the peasant." (Tawfiq al-Hakim, *The Return of the Spirit*, trans. William M. Hutchin, Washington DC: Boulder/Three Continents Press, 1990, p. 272.)

21. 'Hitler's Boyhood', The History Place <http://www.historyplace.com/worldwar2/riseofhitler/boyhood.htm>.

22. Jesse Greenspan, '9 Things You May Not Know About Mussolini', History, 7 February 2019 <https://www.history.com/news/9-things-you-may-not-know-about-mussolini>.

23. Ibid.

24. See: 'Ahmed Hasan al-Bakr', *Britannica* <https://www.britannica.com/biography/Ahmad-Hasan-al-Bakr> and Audiopedia, *Ahmed Hassan al-Bakr* [video], 28 October 2015, retrieved at <www.youtube.com/watch?v=69TqnD8xqhg>.

25. Fuad Matar, *Saddam Hussein: The Man, the Cause and the Future* (Highlight: London, 1981), p. 54.

26. Footage of the purge can be seen online. See, for example: John Simpson for BBC News, *Saddam's 1979 Baath Party purge* [video], 13 December 2013 <https://www.bbc.co.uk/news/av/world-middle-east-25363857/saddam-s-1979-baath-party-purge>.

27. Ibid. A full recording of the events in 1979 can be seen here: Muḥammad al-ʿIrāqī, *al-Mujrim al-maqbūr Ṣaddām Ḥusayn baʿd usbūʿayn min tawallīhi al-ḥukm wa iʿdām rifāqat al-Baʿthiyīn fī Tammūz 1979* [video], [The dead criminal Saddam Hussein two weeks after taking power and eliminating a group of Baathists in July 1979], 13 May 2018, retrieved at <youtu.be/fc9iwL5urDw>.

28. Ibid.

29. Ibid.

30. Ibid.

31. Ibid. A traditional way of addressing an Arab father (or mother) is to call them 'father (mother) of his first son', so here he says: 'Father of Uday'.

32. Ibid.

33. Neil MacFarquhar, 'Saddam Hussein, Defiant Dictator Who Ruled Iraq With Violence and Fear, Dies', *The New York Times*, 30 December 2006 <https://www.nytimes.com/2006/12/30/world/middleeast/30saddam.html>. See also Ahmed Mansour's interview with one of Saddam's ministers, Salah Omar al-Ali: Al Jazeera Arabic, *Witness to an Era* [video], in nine parts, retrieved at:
    Part 1 <https://youtu.be/iyeDZiC481E>;
    Part 2: <https://youtu.be/OTd6uejM0Fg>;
    Part 3: <https://youtu.be/DoE9_HB9VnU>;
    Part 4: <https://youtu.be/02XUBsMVrCI>;
    Part 5: <https://youtu.be/rngkqpJ0Dhw>;
    Part 6: <https://youtu.be/ZSZW5XUek5k>;
    Part 7: <https://youtu.be/gBAQ6V8t_c4>;
    Part 8: <https://youtu.be/8jBGxizY7w8>;
    Part 9: <https://youtu.be/rwzVxXfCvRc>.

34. Ibid.

35. Standard biographical sources confirm their involvement in the formation of the Free Officers. See, for instance, 'Gamal Abdel Nasser', *Britannica* <www.britannica.com/biography/Gamal-Abdel-Nasser>, accessed 2 October 2019, and 'Muhammad Naguib', *Britannica* <www.britannica.com/biography/Muhammad-Naguib>, accessed 2 October 2019.

36. The removal of comrades and the attempt to oust Abdel Hakim Amer is documented in Yosri Fouda's Al Jazeera series *Top Secret* on Abdel Hakim Amer. See: Al Jazeera Arabic, *Part 1: The Death of the Second Man* [video], 26 July 2008, retrieved at <www.youtube.com/watch?v=oGzvCsJfNXs> and *Part 2* [video], 26 July 2008, retrieved at <www.youtube.com/watch?v=qR8FxOIpHWo>.

37. Ibid. See also 'Military prosecutor to investigate death of former Egypt defence minister Abdel-Hakim Amer', Ahram Online, 6 September 2012 <http://english.ahram.org.eg/

NewsContent/1/64/52162/Egypt/Politics-/Military-prosecutor-to-investigate-death-of-former.aspx>.

38. Ibid.

39. Ibid. In addition, see: 'Riyā ibnat wazīr al-ṣiḥḥa alladhī aʿdamahu Ṣaddām ʿam 1982 – mā dhā qālat ʿan abīhā wa kayfiyyat iʿdāmihi' [Riya, the Daughter of the Health Minister Executed by Saddam in 1982 – What She Said about Her Father and How He Was Executed], *Kunūz Media* <https://bit.ly/2PyWMGr>.

40. Dave Gilson, 'The CIA's Secret Psychological Profiles of Dictators and World Leaders Are Amazing', *Mother Jones*, 11 February 2015 <https://www.motherjones.com/politics/2015/02/cia-psychological-profiles-hitler-castro-putin-saddam/>.

41. Dr Jerrold M. Post, 'Explaining Saddam Hussein: A Psychological Profile', presented to the House Armed Services Committee, December 1990.

42. In an interview with Christiane Amanpour, Hosni Mubarak said that if he resigned he was afraid there would be chaos and the Muslim Brotherhood would take over: "Obama is a very good man. But I told Obama, 'you don't understand the Egyptian culture and what would happen if I stepped down right now,'" Amanpour said in a broadcast on 3 February 2011 recounting her conversation with Mubarak. "He said again that there would be chaos and he said that the banned Islamist party, the Muslim Brotherhood, would take over." See Christiane Amanpour, 'Mubarak: "If I Resign Today There Will Be Chaos"', ABC News, 3 February 2011 <http://abcnews.go.com/International/egypt-abc-news-christiane-amanpour-exclusive-interviewpresident/story?id=12833673>.

43. See, for example, a tweet from MBS of Saudi Arabia: "Our country and Saudi citizenship is an honour that traitors do not deserve, and a form of love which agents [of a foreign power] do not feel." [trans. Russell Harris] <https://twitter.com/alminjaf/status/454504470018527232>. See also, in Arabic: Tamarod Australia, *Amīr al-falāsifa Sīsīlāṭūn: al-Sīsī khilāl liqāʾihi biʾl-jāliya al-miṣriyya fī Almāniyā yawm 4 yūniya 2015* [video], [The Prince of Philosophers Sisi-Plato: al-Sisi meets the Egyptian community

in Germany, 4 Jun 2015], 7 July 2015, retrieved at <https://youtu. be/91ClJtZFVq4>.

44. Jane Warren, 'The son Josef Stalin despised', *The Express*, 22 February 2013 <https://www.express.co.uk/news/world/379414/ The-son-Josef-Stalin-despised>. Images of the arrest can be seen online at Rare Historical Photos, 'Stalin's son Yakov Dzhugashvili captured by the Germans, 1941' <https://rarehistoricalphotos.com/ stalins-eldest-son-yakov-dzhugashvili-1941>.

45. Select examples include: Adolf Hitler in a speech about Jews (Empire HD, *Adolf Hitler talks about Jews* [video], 23 August 2016, retrieved at <https://archive.org/details/youtube-IDVup_Pqb2w>); Qaddafi's speech in which he calls protestors rats (SLOBoe, *Muammar Gaddafi speech* [video], 23 February 2011, retrieved at <https://www. youtube.com/watch?v=69wBG6ULNzQ>); and el-Sisi stating that God created him as a doctor who knows how to diagnose national ills (word video, *I'm a doctor – all philosophers and world leaders say people should listen to what this man says* [video], 5 June 2015, retrieved at <www.youtube.com/watch?v=5nitY4-un3E>).

46. Saddam Hussein wept over the death of a health minister and friend who he had executed, according to an account by the Minister's daughter. See: 'Riyā ibnat wazīr al-ṣiḥḥa alladhī aʿdamahu Ṣaddām ʿam 1982 – mā dhā qālat ʿan abīhā wa kayfiyyat iʿdāmihi' [Riya, the Daughter of the Health Minister Executed by Saddam in 1982 – What She Said about Her Father and How He Was Executed], *Kunūz Media* <https://bit.ly/2PyWMGr>.

47. Salwa Alghanim, *The Reign of Mubarak al-Sabah: Shaikh of Kuwait 1896–1915* (London and New York: I.B.Tauris, 1998).

48. 'Riyā ibnat wazīr al-ṣiḥḥa alladhī aʿdamahu Ṣaddām ʿam 1982 – mā dhā qālat ʿan abīhā wa kayfiyyat iʿdāmihi' [Riya, the Daughter of the Health Minister Executed by Saddam in 1982 – What She Said about Her Father and How He Was Executed], *Kunūz Media* <https://bit. ly/2PyWMGr>.

49. Constantin Pîrvulescu's speech can be seen online: Andrei Mihai, *Congresul XII – PARVULESCU CONTRA CEAUSESCU*

[video] 18 October 2006, retrieved at <https://www.youtube.com/watch?v=UXjlz5S0JGQ>.

50. Although Pîrvulescu was 84 years old at the time of his speech opposing Ceaușescu, he lived to see the collapse of Ceaușescu's regime in December 1989. He died in 1992 at the age of 96. See: Vladimir Tismaneanu, *Stalinism for All Seasons: A Political History for Romanian Communism* (Berkeley: University of California Press, 2003), p. 266.

51. Ahmed Abdalla, *The Student Movement and National Politics in Egypt 1923–1973* (Cairo: The American University in Cairo Press, 2008), pp. 152, 158–59.

52. Nasser agreed on 30 March 1968 to hold new elections for the Arab Socialist Union. Elections took place the following year. The presidential address to the nation is available in Arabic here: 'Bayyān al-ra'īs Jamāl 'Abd al-Nāṣir ilā al-umma. Bayyān 30 Mars, 1968' [Gamal Abdel Nassir's Message to the Nation. 30 March 1968] <http://nasser.bibalex.org/Data/GR09_1/Speeches/1968/680330_bayanat.htm>.

53. See, in Arabic: Nagwa Ibrahim, 'Parliamentary Stories: Sheikh Ashour, the Representative that Opposed Nasser, Shaarawi, and Sadat', *al-Taḥrīr*, 27 February 2015 <https://bit.ly/2TNrvgv>.

54. Ibid.

55. Ibid.

56. Ibid.

57. Published only later, Ahmed Fouad Negm's poems were initially put to music and sung by his blind oud-playing companion Sheikh Imam. See: *'Āshūr* [video], words by Aḥmad Fu'ād Negm, lyrics and vocals by al-Shaykh Imām, 16 July 2013, retrieved at <www.youtube.com/watch?v=6Rp3IXN8uJw>.

58. Adel Hamouda, *al-Nukta al-siyasiyya* [The Political Joke] (Cairo: al-Firsan Publishers, 1999).

59. Salah Nasr was the head of the Egyptian General Intelligence Directorate from 1957 to 1967. In addition to running a hated and reprehensible agency that went after political opponents and dissidents, he conscripted actresses to seduce VIPs, who were filmed and blackmailed. Nasser ordered Salah Nasr's arrest and

trial. See: 'On the anniversary of his death, the sexual digressions of intelligence chief Salah Nasr with the most beautiful female celebrities,' *al-Fajr*, 5 March 2017 <www.elfagr.com/2490654>.

60. Examples include: Hosni Mubarak, Saddam Hussein, Muammar Gaddafi and Ferdinand Marcos (see: Nick Davies, 'The $10bn question: what happened to the Marcos millions?' *The Guardian*, 7 May 2016 <https://www.theguardian.com/world/2016/may/07/10bn-dollar-question-marcos-millions-nick-davies>).

61. "The building, which costs a dizzying $6 million a year to run, is still 70% empty." John Malathronas, 'See Nicolae Ceausescu's grandiose and bloody legacy in Bucharest', CNN, 5 December 2014 <https://edition.cnn.com/travel/article/ceausescu-trail-bucharest-romania/index.html>.

62. See: Brian Titley, *Dark Age: The Political Odyssey of Emperor Bokassa* (Montreal and Kingston: McGill-Queen's University Press, 1997), p. 83.

63. See: Patrick Fandio and Edouard Dropsy, *Revisited: The remains of Central Africa Republic's imperial past* [video], France 24, 22 December 2017 <https://www.france24.com/en/20171222-video-central-african-republic-revisited-imperial-past-emperor-bokassa-1st>; see also: Howard W. French, 'An African Ex-Emperor Laments His Reputation', *The New York Times*, 2 June 1996 <www.nytimes.com/1996/06/02/world/an-african-ex-emperor-laments-his-reputation.html>.

64. Titley, *Dark Age: The Political Odyssey of Emperor Bokassa*, p. 91.

65. Daniel Chirot, *Modern Tyrants: The Power and Prevalence of Evil in Our Age* (Princeton: Princeton University Press, 2009), p. 398. The Central African Republic was a poverty-stricken empire under Bokassa, see: Thomas O'Toole. '"Made in France": The Second Central African Republic', *Proceedings of the Meeting of the French Colonial Historical Society*, vol. 6/7 (1982), pp. 136–146.

66. Idi Amin also declared himself King of Scotland. See: Peter Beaumont, 'Idi Amin Dada, VC, CBE .. RIP', *The Guardian*, 17 August 2003 <https://www.theguardian.com/world/2003/aug/17/peterbeaumont.theobserver>.

67. In fact, the removal of such statues often symbolises the end of a dictator's reign. Take, for example, the tearing down of Saddam Hussein's statue in 2003. See John Hudson, 'Down goes the dictator! A visual history of statue vandalism', Foreign Policy, 5 March 2013 <https://foreignpolicy.com/2013/03/05/down-goes-the-dictator-a-visual-history-of-statue-vandalism/>.

68. The volume of shipping traffic through the Suez Canal was not projected to increase, and therefore the investment in its expansion would not generate revenue to cover its costs. Meanwhile, el-Sisi has stated that, "If we only dealt with Egypt by means of feasibility studies we would only have realised 25 per cent of what we have accomplished." See: 'Suez Canal traffic levels show signs of recovery in 2017', The Medical Telegraph, 19 October 2017 <http://www.themeditelegraph.com/en/transport/seatransport/2017/10/19/mercedes-benz-suez-egypt-8pcIpTPS9uFjG7D61u9KjL/index.html>; and al-Yawm DMC [a media organisation], al-raʾīs al-Sīsī yaftatiḥ muntada "Afriqiyya 2018" bi Sharm al-Shaykh [video], [President Sisi opens the Africa 2018 club in Sharm al-Sheikh], 9 December 2018, retrieved at <youtu.be/j5QFgPJ4m2c>.

69. Among the attendees were: French President François Hollande; King of Bahrain Hamed Bin Isa Al-Khalifa; Kuwaiti Emir Sabah Al-Ahmad Al-Jaber Al-Sabah; Saudi Deputy Crown Prince Mohammed Bin Salman; Yemeni President Abd Rabbu Mansour Hadi; King Abdullah of Jordan; Palestinian President Mahmoud Abbas; Sudanese President Omar Al-Bashir; Swiss Vice President Johann Schneider-Ammann. See: Mesrop Najarian, 'Egypt inaugurates Suez Canal expansion', CNN, 7 August 2015 <https://edition.cnn.com/2015/08/06/world/new-suez-canal-opens/index.html>.

70. Marty Wall and Isabella Wall, Chasing Rubi: The Truth about Porfirio Rubirosa, the Last Playboy (Literary Pr Pub, 2005), p. 37.

71. Gabriel García Márquez's The Autumn of the Patriarch, published in 1975, explores just such a virtual world.

72. See: SLOBoe, Muammar Gaddafi speech TRANSLATED (2011 Feb 22) [video], 23 February 2011, retrieved at <https://www.youtube.com/watch?v=69wBG6ULNzQ>.

73. See: Amanpour, 'Mubarak: 'If I Resign Today There Will Be Chaos''.
74. In Zine el-Abidine Ben Ali's final televised address of 14 January 2011, he is heard to say: "I heard you. I heard you all, the unemployed, the needy, the activist, and those who demand greater freedoms…". It is accessible here: Brhoooom2009, *Ākhir khiṭāb li-l-ra'īs al-Tūnisī Zayn al-'Ābidīn qabla hurūbihi li'l-khārij* [video], [The last speech given by the Tunisian president Zine el-Abidine Ben Ali before his flight from the country], 14 January 2011, retrieved at <www.youtube.com/watch?v=3vvjSILioOE>.
75. Footage of Ceauşescu's trial can be accessed online.
76. 'Survivors Describe Massacre in Bangui', *The New York Times*, 30 September 1979 <www.nytimes.com/1979/09/30/archives/survivors-describe-massacre-in-bangui-2-central-africanyouths-say.html>; 'An African Ex-Emperor Laments His Reputation', *The New York Times*, 2 June 1996 <www.nytimes.com/1996/06/02/world/an-african-ex-emperor-laments-his-reputation.html>.

9 Prevention of the dictatorship syndrome

1. For example, a whole two days after the deaths of Coptic Christian protesters at Maspero, the Egyptian military stuck to its line that it did not fire live ammunition, no protesters were run over by military vehicles and no force was used: "This cannot be blamed on the Egyptian Armed Forces. It can be blamed on anyone else. It cannot be written in history that we crushed someone, even in confrontations with the enemy." See: *The military council press conference on the events of Black Sunday* [video], 12 October 2011, retrieved at <www.youtube.com/watch?v=YWJiQlfwz70>.
2. See: Ahmed Abdalla, *The Student Movement and National Politics in Egypt 1923–1973* (Cairo: The American University in Cairo Press, 2008) and Amira Nowaira, 'Egypt 1967 – a very personal defeat', *The Guardian*, 27 May 2010 < https://www.theguardian.com/commentisfree/2010/may/27/egypt-1967-very-personal-defeat>.
3. The following newspaper articles reference the appearance, in Arabic: 'Abd al-Masīḥ Mamdūḥ abd Sayyid Yūsuf, '50 'āmman

alā ẓuhūr al-ʿadhrāʾ fi kanīsat al-Zaytūn' [50 Years since the Appearance of the Virgin in the Zeitoun Church], *al-Youm al-Sābiʿ*, 3 April 2018 <www.elbalad.news/3154049>; Michal Hanna, '2018 ʿāmm iḥtifālāt al-kanīsa wa '1-aqbāṭ' [2018 is a year of celebrations for the Church and the Copts], *al-Balad*, 4 February 2018 <https://bit.ly/2DldTDH>; as does this video report: wsaleeby, *The Virgin Mary Apparition 1968–70 in Zeitoun*, Egypt [video], 6 February 2013, retrieved at <https://www.youtube.com/watch?v=aQFhxp9070s>. See also, in English, Peter LaFave, 'When Mary Returned to Egypt: The Apparition at Zeitoun', The Christian Review, 21 January 2016 <http://www.thechristianreview.com/when-mary-returned-to-egypt-the-apparitions-at-zeitoun/>.

4. Ibid.
5. Ibid.
6. Ibid.
7. See, in Arabic: ʿAmmār ʿArab, 'Ghaṭāʾ al-raʾs ikhtirāʿ ikhwānī' [The veil is an invention of the Ikhwān], al-Ḥiwār al-Mutamaddin [news organisation], 2 June 2018 <www.ahewar.org/debat/show.art.asp?aid=601133&r=>.
8. See: Magdi Khalil, 'The Saudi Influence over Egypt: The long reach of Wahhabism', Frontpage Mag Archive, 11 February 2015 <https://archives.frontpagemag.com/fpm/saudi-influence-over-egypt-magdi-khalil/>.
9. It is also worth noting that Wahhabi religious scholars detail fatwas against opposing a Muslim ruler. See, in Arabic: Ḥukm al-khurūj ʿalā al-ḥakim [Ruling on rising up against a ruler], 25 August 2013 <fatwa.islamweb.net/fatwa/index.phppage=showfatwa&Option=FatwaId&Id=216631>, and 'Hal iqtirāf baʿḍ al-ḥukkām li'l-maʿāṣī wa '1-kabāʾir mūjib li'l-khurūj ʿalayhim?' [Must one rise up against leaders who sin?], website of Shaykh Imam ibn Bāz <https://bit.ly/2QBEHD3>.
10. Ibid.
11. See: 'chauvinsim', Cambridge Dictionary <https://dictionary.cambridge.org/us/dictionary/english/chauvinism>.

12. Hitler can be heard describing the Jewish conspiracy he alleged here: Empire HD, 'Adolf Hitler talks about Jews (Speech)', 23 August 2016 <https://archive.org/details/youtube-IDVup_Pqb2w>.

Acknowledgements

I would like to express my profound thanks to Barbara Schwepcke, whose idea it was in conversation with me for us to work together on a book on this subject, a process I have enjoyed very much. I am grateful, too, to her colleagues Harry Hall and Alice Horne for their insights and careful engagement as the manuscript has been prepared for publication. I would like to thank Russell Harris for his meticulous translation and Abdalla F Hassan for his detailed research and assistance throughout. I am grateful to my literary agents Andrew Wylie and Sarah Chalfant, and their colleagues Charles Buchan (for whose feedback my particular thanks), Jessica Friedman and Sarah Watling. Finally, I would like to thank my valued readers, many of whom may have experienced some of the difficult conditions described in this book – to them I am sincerely indebted, and with them I hope we may all look forward to a dictatorship-free future.

Index

A

Abbasid state, the, 95,
    96–7
Achebe, Chinua, 78
al-Abbas, Abu, 95
al-Assad, Bashar, 29
al-Assad, Hafez, 115
al-Bakr, Ahmed Hassan,
    114–15
al-Berry, Khaled, 101–4
al-Hakim, Tawfiq, 10, 112
al-Sabah, Shaykh
    Mubarak, 106
Al Saud, Abdullah bin
    Abdulaziz, 108
Al Thani, Shaykh Hamad
    bin Khalifa, 106
Amer, Abdel Hakim, 73–4,
    118–19, 122
America see United States
    of America, the
Amin, Idi, 120, 127
Arab Spring, the, 46
Argentina, 7, 70

Asfour, Gaber, 74, 78,

B

Ba'ath Party, 52, 114–17
Baghdad, 28, 96
Ben Ali, Zine El Abidine,
    130
Bokassa, Jean-Bédel, 11, 28,
    36, 127, 131
Bonaparte, Napoleon, 141,
    127
Britain, viii, 7

C

Cairo, vii, 2, 32, 39, 91, 96,
    112
caliphate, 94–5, 96, 100,
    140
Castro, Fidel, 69–70
Ceauşescu, Elena, 9, 130
Ceauşescu, Nicolae, 41,
    123, 126, 130
Central African Republic,
    28, 127

chauvinism, 133, 141–2
Churchill, Winston, 7, 11
Crusades, the, 88, 142

D
Díaz Mori, José de la Cruz
  Porfirio, 109–10
Duvalier, François, 113–14

E
Egypt, vii–viii, ix, 112
  censorship, 1, 47–8,
    58–9
  relations with Syria, 2,
    90–91
  revolution, vii, 46, 107–8
  society, 10–11, 18, 19–22,
    24–5, 32, 34, 55–6, 57,
    61, 139, 140
  war with Israel, 1–7,
    42–3, 137
Eissa, Salah, 81
Elders of Zion, the, 37–8
el-Sisi, Abdel Fattah, vii,
  41, 50, 111, 128
England, Lynndie, 45
Equatorial Guinea, 29

F
First World War, 71, 108,
  109

Francisco Macías Nguema,
  29
Franco, Francisco, 11, 68
Free Officers, the, 49,
  117–18

G
Gaddafi, Muammar, 11, 29,
  36, 41, 74, 76–8, 120, 127,
  128, 130, 131
García Márquez, Gabriel,
  70
Gaza, 5, 43, 100, 118
Germany, 7, 38, 44, 66–7,
  100, 108, 112
Goebbels, Joseph, 50, 65,
  67
Golan Heights, the, 5, 43,
  118
Gramsci, Antonio, 68

H
Haidar, Haidar, 59
Hiroshima, 45
Hitler, Adolf, 11, 38–9, 44,
  66–7, 90, 99, 108, 110,
  111, 112, 131, 142
Holocaust, the, 39, 44, 100
Hussein, Saddam, 11, 28,
  36, 52, 78–81, 110, 114–
  20, 122, 131

Hussein, Taha, 56

I
Iran, 52, 105
Islamic State, 86
Islamism, 39, 45, 46, 58–9,
   93–5, 97, 98, 99–104
Israel, 19, 41
   see also Egypt–Israel War
Israel–Palestine conflict, 2,
   39, 100
Italy, 7, 51, 109

J
Jerusalem, 5, 43, 88, 118
jihad, 94, 95, 100, 140

K
Khomeini, Ayatollah, 105
Khrushchev, Nikita, 72
Krupskaya, Nadezhda, 51
Kuwait, 106, 122, 131

L
La Boétie, Étienne de, 8–9,
   30
Le Bon, Gustave, 86–8
Lenin, Vladimir, 51
Libya, 29, 41, 76–7, 127,
   130, 131,
Lorca, Federico García, 68

M
Mahfouz, Naguib, 72–4
Mann, Thomas, 66–7
May, Karl, 112
Milošević, Slobodan, 111
Monk, Robert the, 88
Mubarak, Hosni, 16–21,
   32, 40, 46, 54, 107–8,
   120, 128, 130
Muslim Brotherhood, 59,
   95, 97, 100, 140
Mussolini, Benito, 11, 52,
   68, 90, 109, 112, 131

N
Naguib, Muhammad,
   117–8
Nasser, Gamal Abdel, 29,
   47–9, 73–4, 90–1, 98,
   122, 123–5, 128, 137
   childhood 110–111, 112
   Egypt–Israel war, 1–11,
      42–3,
   the Free Officers,
      117–19
National Socialism *see*
   Nazism
Nazism, 38–9, 44, 50, 65,
   66–7, 108, 111, 121
Neruda, Pablo, 68–9
Niyazov, Saparmurat, 128

Nobel Prize, 71–2

O
Ottoman state, the, 96

P
Pahlavi, Shah Mohammad
  Reza, 105
Pakistan, 94, 99
Palestine, 2, 39
'Papa Doc' *see* Duvalier,
  François
Paradise Hall Massacre,
  115–16
Pasternak, Boris, 71–2
Pirandello, Luigi, 69,
Pîrvulescu, Constantin,
  123
Portugal, 7, 35
Putin, Vladimir, 42

Q
Qatar, 106
Quddous, Ihsan Abdel,
  49
Qur'an, the, 51, 85–6, 92,
  95, 129

R
Remarque, Erich Maria,
  67

Romania, 41, 123, 126–7,
  130
Russia, 38, 42, 71, *see also*
  Soviet Union, the

S
Salazar, António de
  Oliveira, 11, 35, 110, 113
Saleh, Tewfik, 79–80
Saudi Arabia, 52, 100, 106,
  107–8
Second World War, 4, 7,
  12, 111, 131
Serbia, 111
Sinai, 4, 5, 43, 118
Solzhenitsyn, Aleksandr,
  67–8
Soviet Union, the, 51, 67,
  69, 71–2, 121, 131, *see also*
  Russia
Spain, 7, 68, 86
Stalin, Joseph, 36, 51, 67,
  68–9, 121
Stalin, Yakov, 121
Sudan, 52, 118
Suez Canal, 95, 128
Syria, 2, 29, 90–1, 115

T
Taliban, the, 100
Tolstoy, Leo, 50, 51

torture, 12, 29, 31, 35, 43,
    45, 49, 54, 75, 93, 104,
    122, 136
Trujillo, General Rafael,
    128
Tunisia, 130
Turkmenistan, 129

U
Uganda, 120, 127
United States of America,
    12, 19, 41, 43, 44, 45,
    99–100, 112, 119,
USSR, the *see* Soviet
    Union, the

V
Van Kirk, Theodore
    'Dutch', 45
Vietnam War, 44

W
Wahhabism, 139, 140
West Bank, the, 5, 43, 118
West, the, 12, 24, 25, 71,
    98–101, 103–4, 140

Z
Zeitoun apparition, 137–8
Zia-ul-Haq, General, 99